STOP COLLABORATE AND LISTEN

Developing Impactful HR Partnerships
through Collaboration

TINA MARIE WOHLFIELD

Taylor –
Thank you for
embracing your
inner HR Peacock!
& For supporting
#TheWooReport
we are truly better
together –
#Runite.

Tina Marie
Wohlfield

DEDICATION

To Kirk Jr. and Brent

I dedicate this book to both of you and all the future collaborators, influential leaders, champions of ideation and inspirational peacocks. Embrace your dreams and own your story.

CONTENTS

ACKNOWLEDGMENTS

I am so incredibly grateful for the many individuals who knowingly (or not) inspired this book. For had it not been these amazing individuals who have been a part of my journey – you would not be reading this book right now.

For those of you I have met in my journey along the way, at a conference, in the workplace, over coffee – those of whom I have been a part of your story or you have blessed me with yours– thank you.

To my husband Kirk. - There are absolutely no words that can accurately express my love and gratitude. Thank you for supporting my career, encouraging me to use my HR voice (or leveraging it when you needed it) and having enough faith in me to know that this peacock needed to fly. Your sacrifices to allow me the roadway to seek my path will always be appreciated. #TeamTIMAWO

To Dr. Lee Meadows - the one man (outside of my husband) that has never been afraid to tell me what I needed to hear (not what I wanted to hear). You have guided and help mold my HR career and challenged me to rise above any HR challenge by embracing failure as the best teacher. Thank you for the best organic collaborative discussions over the years, especially during those days I endured that dreadful 696 commute. We have collaborated and engaged ideas on "how" to have dialogue around the most innovative and thought-provoking HR topics. As a fellow Jedi master of organic collaboration - I have mastered and discovered the power of my craft because of you.

To John "Flaco" Kontos - Thank you for being a champion of the HR Community, for believing in me and the efforts of so many HR Jedi before me. You are a master of powerful relationships that enhance collaboration at its finest. I not only cherish your ability to build and establish powerful connections – but the result to which is one of the best friendships and long-standing place within my "circle of trust".

To Gerald Chiddick– Thank you for reminding me that I had a story to tell and continue to remind me why I should be sharing that story with **everyone** (regardless if they want to hear it or not.) You are a true example of servant leadership and a fellow peacock whose insight can empower **any** organization to succeed.

To Kat Lacy-Wilson – Thank you for being a core member of my inner circle and for your **daily** support and encouragement. You inspire me **every day** to embrace diversity and inclusion through the power of collaboration.

To Blanca Fauble – Thank you for opening my eyes to view diversity through ideas and to embrace my inner peacock. You a true inspiration to and an influential woman leader.

To Dr. Rita Fields – Thank you for keeping it real and for being the champion of disruptive HR and the concept of influential leadership. You paved the way for individuals like me to embrace (not fear) collaboration and diversity of thought.

To Tom Daniels – Embrace your inner peacock (or falcon). Thank you for being a part of my journey and for sharing the page in Gladwell's Tipping Point for best example of "Connector". My eviction from the *Change House* is still pending from the *Dungeon of Denial*. I will forever cherish our friendship and the fact we are the best Euchre team ever assembled. #Falconsflyforever

To Sandy Harvey, Dr. Keith Levick, Lisa Parys and Anne Young – Thank you for nudging me to fly and for reminding me that I will not fall. Your support helped make this journey of mine a reality. #WEAREBETTERTOGETHER

To Christine Steinhebel, Gehan ("G") Haridy-Ardanowski, Kristi Stuetzer, Kim Thomas, Marci Rosenberger, Christie Reeves, Feliz Rodriguez, Stephanie Maynard, Greg Modd, Janelle Thomas, Justina Carey, Jennifer Campo and **ALL** the members of the HRUnite! Family – Thank you for your inspiration, your support and being innovators advancing the HR Tribe! #HRUnite!!

To Alora Caminiti, stay the course and embody your passion for HR through action. You are the future of HR and organizations need you and will continue to need you more than you know! #HRPURPOSE

To Tony Moore, thank you for reminding me that the art of storytelling is a true gift and that I need to always walk around the hole in the sidewalk. #THATSCOOL

To my wonderful sons Kirk Jr. and Brent – thank you for being my biggest fans and believing in me. You are always reminding me that collaboration is a gift and that embracing alternative opinions and avoiding judgement is the foundation of any relationship. I love you.

FOREWORD

Life is short. I know this is a cliché' but it is true in the grand scheme of things. Another thing that is true is that many of us spend our time in life marking time vs. making time.

I know this first hand as I feel that I spend any part of any day, week, month or year trying to prioritize what I have to do vs. what I want to do. We all have obligations but we seem to neglect to serve ourselves as we execute in our service of others. This sacrifice is a really important distinction in the spirit of this book. The author is someone who I watched and collaborated with as we worked together and provided a service to others regarding talent development and management. She is also someone who as a professional is highly skilled at developing a collegial trusted dialogue., I find her amazingly capable of communicating value in very common-sense ways that had proven to be transformative. But I noticed as time wore on that there was a story born out of experiences that could be insightful to others if she was willing to take the leap.

As a result of our ongoing talent management and career development conversations we continually came back to the same theme, "what is the purpose of my work and how else can I be of help?" This is a very broad question. Especially when you put the earlier comments into perspective.

My counsel to our author was; tell your story. Tell it in the same collaborative common-sense manner that you have provided business consultative service to me and the company we mutually worked for. Tell it in the same humorous but serious tone that lets the reader know that these experiences they are having in life help shape who we are and how we will be perceived. Lastly tell your story so that the reader can find themselves in parts if not all of it because it is through shared experiences that we normalize our own views and behaviors. When you do this you have helped and you have answered the question. You have also made time and enhanced your life by enriching

The lives of others.

-Gerald Chiddick

The hallmark of any profession is measured by its ability to open portals that allow its talented members to forge a path for others guided by a star whose light can never be diminished. As a dyed-in-the-wool member of the Human Resources profession, I have had the luxury of watching a number of stars bring light to the changes that move our discipline. The star that holds the name Tina Marie Wohlfield is one whose light shines brighter and broader across the Human Resources landscape. Where others speak of 'passion' for a discipline, Tina Marie acts on her passion for the profession and the people with whom she connects. She continues to be a consummate professional who immerses into the experiences of being a Human Resource professional and emerges with deeper and focused insights that help to transform our profession and position it for the uncertain future. Now, the culmination of those experiences have been put to print in a well-written, personal account of the critical truths that move Reaction to Pro-action. STOP! Collaborate and LISTEN! captures one person's journey through the maze of individual and organizational transformation. Tina Marie's documented and insightful perspective on facilitating change will serve as a beacon for Human Resource professionals for years to come. Her journey has been eventful and with the wind in her sails, unstoppable! I cannot wait to see what she will accomplish next!

Lee E. Meadows, Ph.D
Professor of Management
Walsh College
Troy, Michigan

INTRODUCTION

HR and Collaboration? Why Do I NEED to Read this Book?

Welcome to HR Group Therapy.

My name is Tina Marie and I have been a practicing HR professional for over 25 years. Over that span of 25 years I can assure you I have seen and experienced a lot over the span of my career. Every day is a new adventure, challenge and our work is never far from done!

I started my HR career in corporate training for a national restaurant chain called China Coast (which is now defunct) in the mid 1990's. I was in college at the time in Grand Rapids, Michigan, double majoring in music and business. The music aspects of my area of study made it challenging to take evening classes so this role allowed me to channel my inner HR and balance the demands of my class schedule.

As a national chain, each region had a group of position specific certified trainers. Our role was to train new team members at our home location and work with new restaurant management teams to train and assist with new location openings. It was through this role that I first learned that collaboration was a critical professional and life necessary skill and that HR was my passion.

I remember one store opening in the Metro Detroit area that was absolute chaotic during the pre-opening "stress test" (invitee only grand opening celebration). I was supporting the front of the house bar/cashier/host areas and because they held this event on a Friday night, there was an unanticipated number of diners. It was like a frat party gone wrong and a lingering disaster as there were wall to wall people everywhere and up to a 3-hour wait to get a table. In usual situations a 3-hour wait would result in a mass exodus of people leaving. Not this time as the event was free of charge and NO ONE was leaving. So, what does one do to pass the time? They navigate over to the bar area. My poor bartenders were overwhelmed and as you can guess the guests were crabby! They wanted their free drinks!! We needed to so something before this turned into a disaster.

Agility is a core competency in the service industry, so I grabbed a cocktail tray and gathered a group of trainees. In five minutes we came up with a plan. We were going to work the bar and main entrance areas and provide cocktail/beverage service to guests to keep the flow of beverages coming from the bar from complete gridlock. This isn't something that the restaurant typically offered so communication and collaboration were vital to this impromptu solution being successful. This effort required more than my managing from a station. I started weaving through the maze of people and set up individuals to take orders, communicate those orders to runners who shared it with someone stationed to enter the orders at the bar. The drinks got made and then someone would then pick up the completed orders, transfer that order to a runner who would pass it along to the person who was serving in that area of the bar who would then solicit payment. It was like a relay race version of the telephone game. Communication and thinking out of the box allowed us to be agile, flexible and keep many people who would have otherwise left, happy! This was my first true professional experience with how effective collaboration in coming up with a solution, trust and communication resulted in a successful outcome. Our corporate training program was focused on functional and required skills for each job; not on communication, team dynamics and collaboration. It was my first "Aha" moment as that situation I experienced that night (facing an unanticipated huge problem) was one that every organization faces on any given day – especially in the role of HR. Collaboration is one of the most impactful leadership tools.

Shortly after this experience, I switched my major strictly to business. I will always have a passion for music, but the excitement I experienced managing by collaboration during my corporate training role helped me realize that Human Resources was my passion.

1
—

HUMAN RESOURCES IS
MY SUPERPOWER

One of the first questions people tend to ask when they first meet me is, "What do you do?" Once I mention the words *human resources* in a sentence, the generated responses can cover a wide span of reactions. You completely understand what I am referring to, because we have all been there.

It likely goes a little like this: you are at a dinner with friends, and someone you just met asks you what you do professionally. You respond that you work in HR.

"Tina Marie, you work in human resources? Wow, I'm so sorry …" This then starts a long response in which the person shares a personal horror story about an experience she had in dealing with someone in HR. Then she asks either, "What is it like firing people?" or "Why do you like firing people?" After you clarify that is far from fun, the person then tells you that you need to come work at her organization, because her HR people seem to enjoy that process *way* too much.

I started seeing a pattern with those horrible shared experiences that triggered people's strong responses to generalize our profession. These experiences were usually centered around a request for help or information, and our HR peers failed to be accessible or flexible or to engage that interaction with empathy.

Why is it that two words, *human resources*, can leverage power, fear, excitement, dread, annoyance, concern, and overall, a general sense of negative energy? Colorful adjective or noun, the concept of HR and all that it enables (or disables) in an organization is a powerful force. Those responses are common thoughts, fears, and perceptions of HR that don't represent our purpose. HR, when leveraged right, can and will harness the energy and successes of the organization's greatest asset to drive business strategy. We need to change negative perceptions so that organizations embrace all that we are—and those negative experiences are few and far between. This, however, does not imply that our entire profession is filled with a bunch of jerks, because that is far from reality and an urban myth. It's almost like we need our own HR reality show—or chronic movie trilogy to show that the HR of yesterday is not the HR of today.

HR Master Jedi—The Force is Strong in This One

I love the *Star Wars* saga and all the themes interwoven in the movies— well, at least episodes four through eight. (I am not sure what exactly happened when they decided to relaunch that franchise with the prequels.) Luke, Leia, Han, Chewy, and my all-time favorite, Master Yoda—now those were some classic heroes. This love for *Star Wars* and my passion for HR and storytelling has garnered me the title "Master HR Jedi" in my inner circle.

What exactly does *Star Wars* have to do with HR and collaboration? If I had a light saber and the ability to move things with my mind, that would certainly make my job easier when employees start behaving badly. This is more about the force and the dance or balance it creates when working through tricky situations to create solutions.

We can all learn from Luke Skywalker in his quest to harness the force for the power of good and balance the fear of being lured to the dark side. In

HR, if we want to leverage our value for good, organizations must learn to let go of the fear of HR and allow the value of HR the opportunity to work. Collaboration is the equivalent to the force in *Star Wars*. However, unlike in the movies, everyone has the power to use it. Every organization I have had the opportunity to serve required me to step into a situation where there may have been more negative interactions than positive. As Luke leverages the force to solve the plight of those in need, I used collaboration to help impact HR's value through trust and strategic partnerships.

Overcoming the Legacy of Bad Behaviors

Over the course of my career in the world's best profession, I have struggled with overcoming the legacy of information hoarding, policy wielding, and judgment passing that have become part of HR's reputation. These struggles inspired me to share my story and insight so that we as a profession can change that perception to one of strategic advisor and asset. We are great in trying to help others, but sometimes, we need to look within to help our own.

Have you ever sat in a meeting with fellow members of your HR or leadership team and been the last to know critical information that would have resulted in less work or quicker solutions? Have you ever shared an idea, feedback on a policy or process, or insight on a problem that resulted in the rest of your department shunning you? Sometimes this is deliberate or just due to ignorance because others are so focused on their roles that they fail to see opportunities to broaden or partner. In some organizations, that behavior is encouraged, because the department is siloed, and knowledge is job security and power. That mind-set and structure got us branded as the Department of No. We all know that was the HR of yesterday. My view of HR is different. We are not the department of No but the department of impact.

HR has only itself to blame for creating the stigma of the HR Department of No. The fact is that many of my peers fell into HR as a role because of a need or the luck of the draw—they were the last ones left in the building on a Friday at 4:00, and someone had to do it. Most of us embarked on this career path with a passion to take organizations to places HR never imagined. I didn't enter the HR field to be a transactional piece of the employee life cycle or be known as a cleaner, and neither did you.

Reactive HR is cleaning up messes and putting out fires created due to decisions made without us. This environment occurs in organizations that either view HR as administrative in nature or in environments where HR has burned the bridges of partnership. Fighting fires and cleaning up is both mentally and physically exhausting! I learned early in my career that the path to navigating change centers around collaboration and partnerships. That epiphany allowed me to harness the power of HR for enhancing strategic value through organizational partnerships.

I am not sharing insights that are new and mind-blowing concepts or part of a different school of thought. Enhancing our value begins with action.

Over the course of the book, I am going to share concepts that we all know, have heard or tried, and failed at or gave up because we lost our voices. Some of my greatest successes came after butt-kicking, falling-flat-on-my-face failures. Failure is the greatest teacher, and through failure emerges collaborative opportunity—which is why there is a whole chapter dedicated to failure. It is from those aha moments that I established the HR rules of engagement.

HR value is through trust and action. It isn't about the title or the inherent power portrayed when you walk into an office wearing black on a Friday and watch all the employees scatter and run for the nearest exits. It isn't about the fear your mere presence creates. It is not about the access to knowledge or power that you are granted in your role. With two or three clicks, you can enter the realm of restricted-access information and sensitive employee data in the organization. It is about leveraging your knowledge and insight as advisor or partner.

We have another barrier that can creep into the perception of no, and that is the tendency to hoard information. Information hoarding began as a quest and thirst for power, because as HR evolved, that cache of data was often all we saw as our internal value.

Contrary to some urban myths, HR is not an entity but a resource in every organization that deals with humans. In order to interact and engage in our role, we must learn to leverage all aspects of our HR toolkit.

Four critical skills or traits in your HR toolkit will enable your success as an HR strategic partner.

- Collaboration
- Active listening
- Trust
- Empathy

Let's Start with One: Collaboration

Collaboration is everything! Grammatically speaking, it is a noun, which makes collaboration an actual thing. Collaboration is the action of working with someone to produce or create something. It was from collaboration that the business competency of ideation, which is an openness to generating and entertaining ideas, evolved.

Collaboration is an interesting concept when you incorporate it into the HR value equation in organizations. It evolves into an action, which is a verb. It is our biggest opportunity to partner; yet years of legacy and stigma make that concept elusive. When you collaborate in organizations, you redefine the definition and turn a noun into an impactful form of value.

Collaboration requires HR to be flexible and open to alternative perspectives and ideas. We need to step out of our departments and into those we service. This allows us to see things not just from three feet away but one hundred feet out looking in. Collaboration is a powerful relationship skill that allows you to engage either proactively or reactively and approach things not just from a linear perspective (point of view), but also from that of your business partner's or stakeholder's standpoint. Collaboration is not a natural tendency for HR because we tend to be the naysayers of alternative points of view. HR has a longstanding legacy of being linear, inflexible, and the department of No. It takes time to build trust within an organization. Trust allows us the opportunity to hit the reset button. HR is here not to be a barrier to change or a problem but to be a partner for proactive solutions.

Collaboration requires flexibility. My favorite phrase when engaging business partners as an HR professional is, "*We will work through it.*" The word *through* implies a solution or resolution to their problem. The key word to any partnership is the word *we*—not *I*, but *we*.

Collaboration has varied levels of meanings based on how someone perceives the relationship. This doesn't mean we need to be collaborative on everything – but we need to seize opportunities when the environment is right and collaboration is the right approach to a problem or situation.

The traditional HR model is a reactive and precipitative. Traditional HR is a centralized model where interactions are made based on transactional needs during designated trigger points over the course of the employee life cycle. Hire – Payroll and Benefit Events – Termination (voluntary/ or not). The transactional mindset is a department that is viewed as and is operating in an insular task and process mindset. An occasional performance improvement transaction takes place but for the most part the involvement/engagement with employees is limited to administrative/ transactional needs. We can't forget those transactional roots, but we can't solely define our value based on those process related transactions.

Technology made those transactions less personal and most can now be accomplished via employee or manager self-service technologies. Technology, on the other hand, has freed up our time to allow us to do things we had not had the time to engage in. I call this model "HR circa 1997". We have so moved on … or so I keep telling myself.

Technology has helped us be more efficient, provide data to support business decisions and better access on demand for employees. However, traditional HR delivery mindset still remains. We miss so many opportunities to interact to build trust, be accessible and establish relationships but hiding behind the self-service model. We have expansive HRIS/Employee Self Service tools and leave the training to virtual decision tree, job aids and online FAQ's.

In the early 2000's, the concept of the HR Business Partner was born, or was it? This concept has always been there, championed by those who didn't spend their time in organizations to be administrative paper processors or policy police. There just became a growing number of those of us who stood up and posed the ages old questions – "Why", "How" and "What"?

The purpose of my story, my challenge to you and every organization who wants to leverage its greatest asset isn't just geared to those in my profession. Collaboration is a core and critical value for diversity in working groups, leadership and everyday life. I am going to share stories from not just the HR perspective but business leaders who also share this same passion. It is through those experiences, stories and lessons learned that we can continue to grow in strategic partnerships. I thank **every** CEO or Leader that has stood up and embodied the value of partnerships and included HR as an integral part of that process. It is the ripple they created that allowed the evolution of the HR partnership to become a reality.

The other three core traits that every HR advocate needs to engage organizations strategically (active listening, trust and empathy) all enhance the act of collaboration. Without the other three, collaboration cannot take place.

My children are in "awe" and "amazement" of my "**HR Voice**". As like Luke (Skywalker), they see that ability to collaborate as a source of influence and power. It's as if HR can convince anyone that "those are not the droids you are looking for" with a calm voice and a wave of one's hand. It is not the voice, but the way we can communicate through collaborative dialogue that allows our influence. **HR is my superpower, and collaboration is how I influence.**

Going back to my first role in corporate training for China Coast, I learned that collaboration is like a dance.

Restaurants are set up in 2 sections – the front of the house and the back of the house. The front of the house is the customer dining areas (servers, host, bar, food runners) the back consists of food prep/chef/dishwashers etc. Restaurants and food service is a coordinated dance from the time a diner is seated at a table to the time they pay and leave. Each part of the house must work together to ensure timing and accuracy of delivery of their portion of the dance to ensure that diners have a positive dining experience. You have to trust, communicate and respect each part of the wheel or things go south quickly. Flexibility and agility are critical – but collaboration is a must for if one side of the house collapses the entire house goes down in flames. Each side must work together for success. Collaboration is a partnership recognizing the needs of others and working together to solve that needs or identify solutions.

Not only did this role change my career path, but it also provided a second "AHA" moment that changed the way I have practiced my craft ever since. As a corporate trainer, I was required to participate in a training certification class to be certified in the positions I would train. During that course we received training on collaborative communication and change management using Lewin's Change Model. I had just finished my sophomore year in college. I had a basic HR class under my belt so I had a basic understanding of Lewin's theory, but why it applied to this role had me puzzled. However, as a self-declared HR junkie, I will admit that I did get a little excited. It was not until I opened my third store for the restaurant chain that I completely understood why both were critical. We needed to be able to face adversity and adapt to change. In a restaurant, change is constant. The number of customers, timing of orders, requests for menu items, availability of ingredients/products, safety, compliance, staff turnover, customer perceptions/demands and weather. The need to embrace and manage change through collaboration is a theme that has woven itself into my professional career. I equate that moment back at my first experiences in corporate training as the moment which many years later was the trigger for me. Leadership requires one to be flexible, agile and an effective communicator – which are not only critical skills in operating a busy restaurant – but critical ingredients in allowing you to build collaborative partnerships.

A few years after my stint in the restaurant industry, I had this insane quest for knowledge on how organizations function, think and operate. I had just relocated to the Metro Detroit area, and met Kirk (my husband) who was attending Walsh College, a small business school known for Accounting and Finance. I worked in HR at a large Credit Union, which had a very robust tuition reimbursement program. Kirk was enrolled in his first of two graduate degree programs there and shared a lot of his experiences with me. He encouraged me to enroll in their MBA program, which I eventually did.

That moment was another epiphany moment in my professional career. It allowed me to harness my ability to see things 100 feet out and not siloed and linear as what I had been trained or asked to do in prior HR roles. I always wanted to ask "why" but didn't know "how". Having that ability changed the way I viewed and delivered HR value in the organizations I have worked in since. It wasn't that piece of paper that gave me that power; it was how I applied the new-found fluency in speaking the language of the business going forward. You can acquire this language in multiple ways without getting an MBA – just find the right *Jedi Masters* who are willing to share that insight and opportunities to acquire it.

I have identified ten simple adjustments that if applied to an organizations HR service delivery model can influence and enhance strategic value and partnerships. The first step in influencing change, is to identify any barriers preventing that change from becoming a cultural norm. The biggest barrier is us.

STOP COLLABORATE AND LISTEN NOTES

2

THE DEPARTMENT OF NO!

Over the course of history, Human Resources has acquired along the way some great accolades along with some very colorful adjectives and emotional responses to describe what we are and what we do. Some of the great ones I have heard along the way include -

- The Policy Police
- The Grim Reaper
- The Evil Empire
- Debbie Downers
- Dress Code Enforcers
- Attendance and Hall Monitors
- Information Hoarders
- **The Department of No!**
- **@*&^#@*(&^ (censored)**

I could go on, but we have all heard it, said it, and experienced it. It's that awkward moment when you meet someone for the first time (or in casual conversations) and they ask you what you do professionally. Then that moment of awkward silence and "I'm sorry". Look, we brought that upon ourselves through legacy actions unintentional as it was. We hid in our offices and remained invisible to the common class of employees. We wore black and when we did come out, walk into departments at 3:00 pm on Friday's, walked into a conference room and shortly after two would enter yet only one would leave. Not only do employees fear us, managers AVOID us. This is **NOT** how the HR story is going to end, at least on my watch. We have the power to own our story – so let's not let the past define the current and future stories yet to be told.

Overcoming the Department of No can **only** be achieved through action. But first we need to understand how we got here to begin with.

Human Resources has a very nasty reputation for being policy hiding, inflexible, reclusive information hoarders. I continually ask those I engage with in the business community about their expectations when working with HR (either as an employee or partner) and the consensus expressed is that of low expectations. "I call HR only when I absolutely have to. Why bother when they are just going to tell me NO."

No one wants to engage with a dance partner that never wants to dance and sit in a corner with their arms folded. This stigma of "no" is a missed opportunity to build a collaborative partnership in the organization because it displays we lack a desire, need or understanding of what the organization needs or wants.

Scene – A Company Conference Room

Manager: "We are trying to establish turnover trend data. Can you share overall trends by department for the XYZ report?"

HR: "NO! I am sorry that information is classified."

Manager: "Why?"

HR: (cricket sounds and a blank stare)

Scene – A Company HR Office

Manager: "James is a rock star employee and our highest performer in the division. James has requested to work remote two days a week due to a long commute related to the long-term construction project impacting the area. The work he does can be easily done remotely."

HR: "No, I am sorry our current policy does not allow us to accommodate his request."

Manager: "Can we review this policy? James is a high performer, former employee of the year and in our leadership development program."

HR: "No"

Fast forward 30 days and James resigns for an opportunity with more flexibility and work/life balance.

The answer isn't automatically yes. When someone engages us with a question, or problem this is our opportunity to start building a partnership through dialogue. The first response before no should always be "Why" or another data gathering question beginning with "What" or "How".

To solve a problem, identify a solution or create innovation. We need to gather data and understand the rationale behind the need.

Let's explore the contributors that may have played into the perception that we only have one word in the HR vocabulary.

Lost in Translation

One of the common reasons that HR has gained the reputation of the Department of ."No" is not because we don't desire to partner or be inclusive. It is that we don't know how to speak the language of the business enough to understand what the request means **or** how to ask the right questions to respond. We **"can't"** or **"won't"** because **"we don't know, what we don't know"** or do not understand the environment internally (and externally) around us. Let's move on to the other contributors to this problem.

No - The Default Response

My curiosity to learn and grow is often satisfied through reading. One of the managers I had the pleasure to support, named Susan, was also an avid reader and she would tip me off to some great reads that she also shared with her team. Susan tipped me off on a must read called "The One Thing" by Gary Keller and Jay Papasan. I have read some of Gary's other published books, so I was very excited to read this one as well. *I highly recommend this book to everyone!*

In the book, Gary talks about how when we are mentally exhausted and fatigued, we tend to resort to our default response of NO. He shared some specific research supporting this rationale in the book that helped me connect this issue to my life interactions. I can think of many situations that I professionally encountered where I was forced to answer "No", not because I didn't want to partner, but because I didn't have the resources, time or energy. I was mentally exhausted. My HR resource capacity was broken due to the fact I was continually "fighting fires" and "cleaning up".

Think of a typical day in your life in HR, regardless of what level you are in your organization. Every day is a new adventure. As the demands and needs of the organization change, our capacity in how OUR resource is being utilized will change with it. If we are spending our time continually fighting fires, or spending all our days in meetings, our mental stamina will be impacted. Even the smartest and greatest leaders fall prey to this condition at some point in their professional lives. Collaborative engagement as a strategic resource will allow us to stave off fires before they flare up and improve your mental stamina, so we have more time to say YES. The more we allow ourselves to be accessible and open to collaborative partnerships, the less fires we are likely to have to face and clean up.

INFORMATION HOARDING

Information hoarding is the one contributing factor that has done the most damage to our internal reputation. It can be either deliberate or unintentional and the after effects long lasting. HR as a profession has a risk management and compliance side. There is a need to be protective, but sometimes we tend to over compensate and hoard information due to fear (protectionism) and power.

Information can be leveraged as an important tool to build trust and create collaborative opportunities. In a prior organization, I was working with a Vice President on a temporary assignment (18-24 months in duration). Functional leadership had identified that this temporary role could be a great development opportunity for someone to gain operational experience outside of their normal functional area. This role would be a platform for future higher-level leadership development focused on specific competencies including customer engagement, industry knowledge and project development. My leader was having dialogue with a peer VP who had a direct report that was identified as high potential and was being considered for higher level opportunities. The individual they were discussing lacked expertise in the hiring leader's area of functional operations. The two leaders had a productive dialogue on how this opportunity may be a great developmental fit. The hiring VP reached out to me and another HR colleague (let's call her Jane) via email for insight on how to navigate exploring this solution further as the organization had never approached development in this manner.

During the request for assistance, the leader requested information related to the identified employee's performance, including assessments and past performance appraisals.

Now based on the situation above – what would your natural reactive response be to this request?

Now, let me describe how this situation played out.

Jane got extremely defensive and quickly responded "No, we do not provide this information for a non-direct report."

My response:

"Hi Joe, I am happy to assist you with this request. Can we set up a time to discuss further? I am not available today due to an offsite meeting but am available on Friday to meet. Jane has worked with this individual directly in a business partner capacity and her insight may be valuable in relation to your request. Jane, can you provide any insight to Joe? He is considering Sue for a developmental stretch assignment in his area."

Email response from Jane to me:

"I have concerns regarding this request and sharing this information with Joe. I do not know what role he is going to consider Sue for, we need to discuss."

The next day, I had a conversation with Jane who was less than agreeable that I was going to provide the information to Joe and my request for her to participate in the process. She was so focused on the **no** that she didn't read the email request asking for her insight. Rather than asking Joe follow up questions on the nature of the request and what he was seeking (why, what or how), Jane jumped to conclusions and passed judgement. This again was a potential missed opportunity to collaborate.

I clarified with Jane that we would not provide him directly with the requested information but what he was seeking was our insight and dialogue to determine if his role would be a good developmental fit for both his needs and the individual being considered. Communication and additional dialogue with a business partner can isolate the "**why**". What he didn't need was all the traditional data to predict future performance, he was looking for the performance behaviors – which he and Sue's direct reporting leader were having dialogue on. Our insight in how to engage Sue to establish how those behaviors fit in his role (and her development needs) was exactly how leaders should engage HR in the process. Ultimately, I may not have changed my colleague's perspective – she is the classic case of information hoarder. I, however, seized the opportunity to collaborate with Joe to meet his business needs and reflect the value of HR as a collaborative partner.

Another example of how information hoarding creates un-necessary barriers featured in the story of "Hidden Figures". One of the main women featured in the story (and subsequent movie) was Katherine Johnson.

Katherine Johnson was a trailblazer and champion of collaboration during the early years of the NASA space program. Her role at NASA was in the mathematical computers department and her collaborative success resulted in calculating the trajectory for entry/re-entry points for critical missions in the space program. If you have read the book, or seen the movie, you will remember the scene in which information hoarding nearly impacted our ability to safely reach and return from space.

During a critical assignment that she was recently assigned to, Katherine is given information that is redacted and missing the necessary data to perform the functions of her job. The answer when she questioned why the data was missing was that she "did not have the proper clearances" and could not be provided the information. She continued to ask why regardless of the response of no. With every request she validated the need with the support on how doing so will have direct value to business strategy and results. Lesson learned - instead of being so reclusive with our data we need to start asking the right questions. Instead of answering NO first– remember to ask those follow up data gathering questions of "**How, What and WHY?**"

The reasons and causes of information hoarding vary. In some cases, it is not malicious intent but a result of over protection/controls regarding information sharing (such as the example described above). In some cases, knowledge hoarding is perceived as power. The more I know, the more powerful position I hold which then results in more job security or influence in the organization. The nature of the information to which we have access to in HR is sensitive in nature and requires a degree of confidentiality and maturity. When knowledge and information hoarding overrides a legitimate business reason for sharing information, it creates barriers to collaboration. The fear of sharing or quest to hold knowledge as power often results in HR factions fighting against each other, rather than partnering for the common good. The circle of trust becomes jaded. Information hoarding impacts the internal department brand and discourages all the natural reasons why the business should engage HR as a partner and strategic resource.

I had the honor and pleasure of speaking at MI HR Day on this very topic. MI HR Day is one of my favorite days in Michigan, as it is a state designated day to celebrate the HR profession and the Michigan HR Tribe gathers at the state capital for a day of professional development.

After my session, an attendee came up to share some of her frustrations on internal information hoarding. She told me that during the presentation it was if I was describing her internal HR department. She worked with a notorious department of information hoarders. In her role, she conducted all the exit interviews for the organization and was responsible for turnover metrics including identifying current and emerging trends impacting turnover. The business partners and recruiters decline to share information with her which could proactively identify potential factors influencing turnover <u>before it occurs</u>. She often heard about issues after an employee has already resigned and has left the organization. When she has brought this up to department leadership, including the business partners and recruiters – they continue to fail to see the value in sharing this information with her. In short, they fail to see how the value this collaborative opportunity will have on the organizations overall strategy. This is a perfect description of those instances where we can see it from 100 feet away, but those in the mix that have the problem never think it's a problem, until it happens to them. So rather than call out their information hoarder behavior, let's continue to find ways to tie it back into the business.

I have learned through my HR experiences that information hoarders often tend to be data geeks. In this situation, my suggestion to her was to tie it back on how your identifying these problems can impact employee retention. This helps the recruiters better manage their open job requisitions and the department HR leader have more positive HR Key Performance Indicators (e.g. reduced turnover, higher engagement scores/productivity, quality of hire) which equates into revenues and ultimately flows directly into the organization strategic goals.

Simple right? Tell only what we need to, for those that need to do it, <u>for a legitimate business reason</u>. When HR functions as precipitative or tactical in nature, we only see things insular as they relate to that task or associated process. We miss the bigger picture opportunity that sharing information or ideation would create.

Information hoarding is a curable. Smart collaboration can help us overcome that image hurting our internal brand.

The Circle of Trust

I was in an office with an HR colleague (for the sake of this discussion, let's call her Katie). Katie and I were discussing an employee relations issue involving a leader who lacked the required leadership skillset for their current role. This leader was being asked to take a new technical role with no direct reports.

Stop here! Before you pass judgement (we talk about judgement later), organizations are notorious for putting managers in leader roles who should NOT be leaders. **HR's role in those situations is to "work through the aftermath" <u>without</u> passing judgement.

Another member of the extended HR team who was not directly impacted or involved in this process, entered the office and asked what we were talking about. Due to the nature and sensitivity of the issue we were discussing, I stopped talking. Unfortunately, Katie continued to repeat **<u>all</u>** the details (plus some) to the person that just joined us. Our conversation turned into a judgement laden gossip tirade as the individual that joined the conversation gave their own opinionated and completely inappropriate response related to the issue being discussed.

As this was going on, I waited for a few moments and then left the office without saying a word. First and foremost, the information being shared with Katie should not have been shared outside the "circle of trust" to which the individual who walked into the office was NOT a member. Regardless of the lack of membership in the circle, the response by both Katie and the other individual contributes to the barriers we face in trying to build collaborative partnerships. We need to avoid judgement and be able to trust that the information we share will be handled with trust and confidence that it will not be used against us.

HR can be a lonely place. It doesn't have to be. You can have personal and productive relationships with others in the organization if you set boundaries. I equate this to dating. When I first started dating, my father made it very clear to any young man that I brought home (and to my now husband) that there are areas/things that are off limits and that no man should cross them. These were the rules of engagement for anyone that wanted to date me.

All collaborative partnerships must have boundaries to establish trust and credibility, specifically ones involving HR. When I have a conversation with an employee/manager or anyone, I establish the rules of engagement pretty quickly. This conversation is a safe place. However, if I need to share this information discussed outside of this conversation, I will be transparent and let you know. I earn trust as my actions reflect that promised commitment.

Trust and credibility are intertwined. We earn trust through action. This means that if I am working on an issue with one department, I do not share all the details with their peers; who upon gaining that knowledge could leverage it against them.

Avoid the Hook – Gossip is Unbecoming of HR

I was part of a conversation with a member of the strategic leadership team related to a business request requiring review and approval by another internal department. The meeting was also attended by another member of the HR team, Nancy. During the course of the conversation, Nancy began to share non-relevant commentary about a member of the other department who had concerns related to that the request. The leader and Nancy began having a judgmental conversation on the person questioning the decision. The conversation then evolved into a discussion about the other department and all their "issues". What began as a productive conversation regarding the status of a pending decision, turned into a gossip filled rant between Nancy, a member of the HR team and a C-level leader. The items being discussed had nothing to do with the business request to which started the conversation and like the example provided before evolved from bias and judgement.

HR is and can become a go-to source for organizational intel. The issue occurs when HR leverages that information in a manner that negates the partnership value HR should have with the entire organization. Keep in mind that if your business partners know you are a loose and quick source for dirt on other departments (like the example I just gave with Nancy), they likely have concluded you are not trustworthy to hold their secrets within the circle of trust. When situations like that occur, those are the individuals we often keep at arm's length because they cannot be trusted. Their paranoia to know information creates a separate set of challenges as information hoarding often results in their wanting information from you – but not reciprocating the dialogue and sharing of information back.

Another type of information hoarding occurs when someone has an obnoxious need to know everything but fails to reciprocate sharing information with others. Ultimately, they expect you and everyone else to share information, but refuse to share it unless it has a direct benefit for them. This is just as bad, if not worse, as oversharing.

These are the individuals that want to know EVERYTHING and when they do know something that can be beneficial to you or anyone else – they keep it close, on lock down. As a collaborative soul, engaging with these types of individuals can be like kryptonite, especially when you become wise to their M.O.

I was once told by a leader that I was not collaborative because an information hoarder peer got mad at me because I only shared with them what they needed to know (not what they wanted to know). Be wary of those individuals, but don't fall prey or change your approach simply because **they** have an "information hoarding problem". Remember, don't bite the hook.

Keep in mind this is a small segment of our HR peers and not the norm. Unfortunately a small few can result in our internal business partners assuming we are all like the rest. These "few" are barriers to collaborative partnerships and these barriers are created by fear.

We can overcome some of that awkwardness early by establishing the HR rules of engagement with a new relationship or business partner. You just need to set boundaries. Setting boundaries establishes your trust and credibility and shows your expectations of integrity. Once those boundaries are established, it is easier to engage in a collaborative partnership. You will always have those individuals that will test your relationship to see if you are like the "others" but setting the boundaries early sets up the stage for constructive dialogue vs office paparazzi.

Information hoarders may not realize or recognize their behavior until it backfires. Sometimes information hoarders purposely withhold information because knowledge is power and in a turn of fate that decision backfires. This effect is also commonly referred to as "karma".

Imagine this scene in an organization conference room at any company.

You and several HR colleagues are sitting in a room with leaders discussing talent strategies within a business unit.

A leader turns to you and asks for your opinion on an ongoing communication issue in one of the areas you support that has escalated and has now made its way to departmental senior leadership. The issue is the result of a disagreement between two leaders and internal service being provided. This is the first you have heard about the issue due to the fact it was initially reported to a colleague notorious for information hoarding. After a ten-minute conversation, due to your relationships with those involved, you are quick to identify that the issue is a result of a communication breakdown between the two departments. The dispute is a result of a prior disagreement between members of the two teams that has created some lingering sensitivity. If the information had been shared or you had been consulted sooner, your knowledge of the dynamics of both teams and their communication styles could have brought a quicker resolution to the situation prior to it escalating to senior leadership. You speak to both leaders involved and set up a focus group of team members to discuss their concerns with a non-biased individual to be a liaison between the two departments.

Your colleague is fuming due to your intervention and resolution and complaining that you are not collaborative to anyone that will listen. Their failure to share information with you hoping your failure to act will make them look better only highlighted how failure to collaborate eventually catches up to those who information hoard. As organizations wake up to the "information hoarding" epidemic, I am hopeful that stories such as those shared will become those telling of lessons learned.

STOP COLLABORATE AND LISTEN NOTES

3

THOU SHALL NOT PASS JUDGEMENT

HR has a reputation for holding grudges and passing self judgement upon all who fail to walk the fine line of policy and compliance. In fact, not only can we be judgmental on others outside of our department, but we are most judgmental on those on our team and within our profession.

LET IT GO

We have all experienced aspects of judgement over the course of our professional career. In HR, sometimes we find ourselves being labeled judge and jury. We all have stories we can share of that "one" manager. You know, the one who when you see them calling, walking into your office, or see a meeting request, you cringe. Why? Because one time, five years ago, that manager made a wrong decision to which you had to clean up? Maybe the manager lacked social/emotional intelligence or communication skills or just made a wrong decision. Maybe the organization failed them by not enabling them with the proper tools to be a leader. Regardless of the reason, it is not our role to judge, but advocate. At the end of the day, regardless of the reason or what choices or actions that manager has taken in the organization, we need to set aside our own personal biases and seek ways to partner to resolve or advocate for the employees to which they interact, manage and influence. The art of management and leadership has a foundation based on the experiences and human interactions that each individual has encountered in their life (personal and professional). If they are not provided an environment to learn the how – then they will continue to be "that" manager and leave a path of devastation and future "that" managers in their wake. Of course, there are situations to which the actions of "that" manager warrant the appropriate response. We should not judge or base biases on decisions or actions that a manager or leader made, and either leaned from or was never provided feedback that the decision was not the best direction to take. **Failure, the greatest teacher is.**

We cannot place blame on an employee when the organization is to blame for putting them into positions to which they are not equipped to handle. We, however can be an advocate for a collaborative solution. Yes, every organization has their fair share of idiots and jerks, but someone hired them. Which means we need to find a way to work through it until they burn the building down or you can rehabilitate them and grant them the feedback and skills they need to be a manager of people. Once a manager becomes labeled as one of <u>"those"</u> managers, we often shut down, avoid them and punish them even long after they have recovered, rehabilitated or paid back their perceived behavioral debt to the organization.

Labeling has "unintended" long term consequences. "Those" managers will avoid you because you create a boundary of "AVOIDANCE". Rather than having a proactive and collaborative partnership, they only call you when the building is on fire and then you must work 100x harder to clean up the aftermath.

"Those" managers are the ones that have influence in the organization because they are loud and often the "squeaky" wheel. Avoidance equates into missed opportunities and louder growing ranks of "naysayers" in the organization. They also continue to spawn additional "those" managers and therefore the vicious cycle continues.

"Those" managers sometimes grow up into great managers and senior leaders, who have more influence than the naysayers and will partner and surround themselves by those that do **<u>not</u>** judge. Those that judged will be replaced by those that seek ways to continue to work together without judgement and diversity.

We miss critical opportunities to collaborate because we can't let go or have the nerve to provide critical feedback when encounters go wrong, or people's feelings are hurt.

Case in Point

I was conducting an employee relations investigation involving several employees. During the information gathering process, I had instructed two individuals involved to not engage with anyone else, including others involved in the investigation. Unfortunately, two employees did not understand what the word "engaged" and "confidential" meant and they immediately began talking to other witnesses. We addressed it immediately and, after a thorough review, took appropriate action. The department leader who initially reported the incident reached out to me and passionately expressed their discontent with how the investigation was being handled (e.g. as my boys would say – that person was "triggered" – which means yelling/screaming and pretty pissed off). I acknowledged their concerns and point of view and, in this case, we agreed to disagree. This was not the first time this leader had reacted in a similar manner, but the first with me. Rather than pass judgement and place this individual on the HR black list, I gave feedback and when they calmed down, we talked about it. They asked me if we were "okay" and I said yes. What this leader needed was feedback on the tone and the way they communicate, not alienation and judgement from their HR business partner.

I had just joined an organization and was beginning to establish my relationships. I appreciate everyone's opinion but always base mine on first-hand accounts and the opportunities any interactions I have can lead to or enhance those relationships further. I was quickly provided the HR rundown on which department heads were difficult, jerks, reclusive, rogue or refused to engage HR. The fact that my counterparts had already labeled, judged and written off over half of the organization was concerning. It also explained why my department had such a negative image in the organization. Passing judgement clouds our ability to be an advocate and lose focus on what value we can bring to the organization through partnerships. That person may be an ass, over emotional or a horrible leader but badmouthing and complaining about them behind the shroud of HR secrecy doesn't solve the problem. It only compounds it.

Judgement can also result in unnecessary drama. I was at an offsite meeting with members of the organization and my team. My counterpart and I received an email complaint from the CEO about an employee wearing "Birkenstocks". The employee in question was a high performer and always dressed professional exceeding the company guidelines of business casual. The email was sent by our higher-level leader and my counterpart immediately began making comments to others about this individual without having all the facts (no empathy/rush to judgement). As my counterpart was preaching her opinion on the issue to anyone who would listen, I jumped in with a comment about their rush to judgement and that considering the individual in question there is likely a reason for the attire.

Before we jump to conclusions, we need to gather enough facts without bias. I called the employee's leader, who was somewhat put off that I even had to make that call (understandably so). The leader explained that the employee broke three of her toes and was unable to wear traditional shoes due to the swelling and impact to her ability to walk. She had an important offsite charity event with several key external stakeholders and had stopped by the office to pick up some materials for that event. She had discussed the issue with her leader and the request to wear open toed comfortable casual sandals was a minor request (and easy to accommodate). Unfortunately, what transpired by members of my team and several members of senior leadership was a rush to judgement and labeling of a high potential employee as a rule breaker. In that specific organization, the culture embraced judgement and had issues with the concept of "Let it Go". Cultural bias, when it is that rampant, is really hard to change. Even in those situations, we all have a voice and this employee needed someone to share their story in the right way – not as water cooler gossip or judgement -but with the facts as they were.

So rather than fall in line with my internal peers, I did what any HR Jedi would do – I provided all the **facts** surrounding the "**why**" to all concerned parties. Unless we advocate for the truth, the perception due to judgement would prevail. In this situation regardless of how I presented it, all that leadership will continue to remember is the one day that this employee wore Birkenstocks – not all the hard work, dedication and impact her efforts have had on the organization.

Organizations that struggle with judgement will most commonly exhibit a fear of failure and other underlying issues as a result.

I was having a conversation with a higher-level leader in that same organization about their own continued development. We discussed the concept of "Fast Fail" and how vulnerability allows a leader to learn and grow from mistakes. The leader expressed concerns that the organization's culture did not support this concept. Success was evaluated based on accomplishments. Failure, no matter how productive the result, was always viewed negatively regardless of how much time transpired since the failure occurred. Fear of failure and judgement inhibits collaboration because the need to succeed results in criticism, stifling of alternative approaches and opinions and complacency. It also impacts the organizations ability to be agile in reaction to changes in both the competitive and external environment to which they exist.

What is agility and why does it matter?

Collaboration enhances the organizations ability to be agile through innovation, ideas and diversity of thought. When there is a fear of failure, collaboration is stifled, and agility is nearly impossible. Without collaboration, leaders become complacent, because those that take necessary risks or innovate change are ostracized in the event of failure or chased out like a peacock in the land of penguins.

Good organizations fail to become "great" or die because of their lack of agility. This is due to complacency, analysis paralysis and being stuck in the status quo due to traditions and fear of failure. In 2018 alone, we saw the demise of Toys r Us and Sears, both long standing retail giants who built the landscape and foundations of the childhoods of so many of us. In each situation, they ultimately met their demise due to their inability to be agile or be open to innovative ideas in the way they did business. I will never forget seeing the picture of "Geoffrey the Giraffe" standing in an empty and desolate store. It is a great reminder to all of us that if our focus is solely insular (internal HR), we lose sight on what's going on around us. When we lose site and connection to our external environment, our internal stakeholders move on without us. HR needs to be agile and evolve just as much as organizations need to evolve to remain a vital and sustainable business.

ANALYSIS PARALYSIS

A lack of agility is often a result of a condition known as "Analysis Paralysis" – the ability and fear to make decisions claiming the need for more data or discussion to act. Traditional HR is a contributor to this organizational epidemic and we need to stop.

Have you ever been in a meeting where you are trying to implement something – it could be the decision to change something as simple as the location of the coffee machine in the office. You have had three meetings to discuss the change including all necessary stakeholders (facilities, the employee committee and leadership). The suggestion to change the location was based on feedback from the employee survey and internal suggestions. You are ready to implement the change which would result in moving the coffee machine five feet on a table to make it more accessible. A viable plan is outlined yet no one is comfortable enough to make a decision to approve the request and therefore a fourth meeting is scheduled.

In the HR world, analysis paralysis is created and embraced by our actions every day. It is a result of our information hoarding and being comfortable sharing appropriate amounts of data to support business decisions within the scope of our confidentiality oath. It is also due to the fact departments will fail to ask us for data, assuming our standard answer is always no. On the flip side, it's not that we don't want to share – we just don't know or understand the how. We don't understand what the business is asking or why (they need it). Our inability to understand inhibits our ability to know what information is needed or how to present the data being requested (HR Analytics is the future of our profession friends better embrace it now).

Analysis paralysis can also occur when organizations over collaborate because of fear of failure or being overly data obsessed. Data obsession creates the environment where a thirst for data can never be quenched and decisions slow or cease because of that continually need to seek more data to support or oppose the direction being considered.

Sometimes we can be our own worst enemy!

The more we understand and can speak the language of the business, the less Analysis Paralysis becomes an issue. It is a chronic epidemic in many organizations – and collaborative dialogue is one way to help tame the thirst for data obsession.

STOP COLLABORATE AND LISTEN NOTES

4

PEACOCKS IN THE LAND
OF PENGUINS

I have had the honor of teaching HR at my alma mater, Walsh College of Business in Troy, Michigan since 2008. Over the course of my years of teaching, I have had the absolute pleasure to meet some amazing individuals who allowed me to be a part of their professional journey. Many of these same individuals have had a powerful impact on my journey along the way. Blanca Fauble is one of them. Her journey has spanned the globe with fortune 500 companies and her own entrepreneurial ventures. Her insight, passion and leadership style embraces diversity. Blanca shared with me a remarkable story about diversity and inclusion by Barbara Gallagher Hateley and Warren H. Schmidt called "A Peacock in the Land of Penguins".

In short, in the land of penguins, you need to talk, dress, act and behave like everyone else. The land of penguins can be described as assimilated to group think regarding ideas, customs and consensus. Those that are different are pushed out and shunned. Either become a penguin or face the isolation of being alone or banished. Peacocks are those that are outwardly vibrant, passionate and innovative. Peacocks stand out in a crowd, even when they try hard not to. The core message is that we need to value and embrace those who are different.

It was from that story I learned I was an HR peacock (or "peahen" if one is to be gender correct). I embraced the concept of collaboration long ago in my HR career and continually sought out professional opportunities which enabled me to share ideas and create powerful partnerships. Sometimes those opportunities were welcome, others took time to nurture and develop - sometimes not at all. In several professional instances, I found myself surrounded by penguins who valued structure, task and processes verses consultative collaboration and partnerships in the delivery of HR services. At times, I found myself lost, on an island set adrift by my own peers who fought to ignore these opportunities with information hoarding, judgement and a lack of inclusion. It was in these moments that I began to look at diversity and inclusion from a different lens. Organizations need a diverse mix of penguins, peacocks, pigeons and birds of all kinds for organic collaboration to happen. This is true diversity. When we surround ourselves with those who think, act, look and speak like us, we chase away the best opportunities to enable positive partnerships to evolve.

Even in those situations where collaboration was not valued by my peers, I did not allow these challenges to sway my passion to seek ways to partner strategically. The highs and the lows in working in organizations where this was embraced or discouraged allowed me to reach the conclusion that in organizations engrained in legacy, where change and alternative ideas are feared, HR is viewed as transactional in nature.

Many organizations, due to the strong legacy of perception and fear of change grasp onto the delivery HR as a push service –transactional in nature. We tell you what to do and you **will** do it. If you don't do it, there will be consequences and you will feel the wrath of HR like no other. HR and the fires to which our profession were born, evolved out of transaction and administrative need. We were created to be precipitative in nature (task and process oriented). The evolution we experienced has changed that, but yet we find ourselves still inclined to hide behind policies, regulations and compliance. I find that rationale to be the land of penguins. The evolution of a strong strategic partnership is centered around a mix of penguins, peacocks and pigeons. I embrace change – maybe it is the OD (Organizational Development) in me that harnesses the power of innovation and change as needed areas of growth in any organization. I have found in my professional career that when in a land of penguins, peacocks are needed and should be embraced, but when organizations fear change they chase them out.

Diversity is the first step in collaboration as it requires one to be open to new ideas, flexible and agile in solutions. When you hide behind policies and compliance – you miss that opportunity to ask "how and why". It isn't that a leader wants to do something that blatantly goes beyond what is allowable – they are ultimately seeking a solution to a problem. Dialogue will allow us to isolate what they are facing/trying to fix/improve or enhance which lends to solutions within the scope of policies, procedures or compliance. Sometimes the policy is the barrier – because it was written in 1998 and no one questioned it then or those that did were peacocks that were banished. Fear is often our biggest barrier. Maybe the answer is still no – but at least those you engaged with in the process recognize your openness to understand their point of view and try to find a palatable solution. THIS my friends is the true spirt of collaboration!!

I am so eternally grateful for interactions on my professional journey that connect me with thought leaders like Blanca. It was a defining moment for me as I had struggled with the frustrations of being shunned and continually sought opportunities to which I could leverage influence among my peers and in organizations through partnerships and collaboration. It also allowed me to embrace my inner peacock and seek out like minded individuals who wanted to change the perception and delivery of HR services making it less about "HR" and more about the business.

Peacocks thrive in collaborative environments where alternative ideas are encouraged and welcome. They value traditions but love seeking ways to enhance and belong.

In HR, we are all naturally inclined to be penguins due to our need to manage risk and compliance – and follow the rules. It's finding that balance between risk and partnership which diversity allows us to recognize there is a little bit of peacock, penguin, pigeon and ostrich in all of us. In a true collaborative flock, penguins understand when it's time to become a taller louder penguin and peacocks know when to showcase their penguin heritage.

It took me a while to identify that one can wear both the penguin and peacock hats based on need and relationship. I was able to accomplish this by learning to embrace my inner peacock and surround myself not just with those similar ideas but penguins, pigeons and an occasional ostrich. I have learned that every organization needs penguin's as much as they need peacocks and other birds to thrive. If the organization was a land of peacocks and in walked a penguin, the result would be the same. Collaboration needs a diversity of ideas, thoughts, trust and partnerships to enable the process to emerge successful.

STOP COLLABORATE AND LISTEN NOTES

5

EMPATHY IS MY SUPERPOWER

Empathy is a necessary core competency of any leader and those in the HR profession. Having the capacity to acknowledge and understand how someone feels or may perceive (viewing from their perspective) allows a leader to build trust and credibility with an audience. Empathy allows HR the ability to be an unbiased advocate on behalf of both the organization and employees. Empathy, however, is an elusive trait that many think they have, yet sympathy is what they show.

Over the course of this book, I have shared several "aha" moments that have defined and shaped my career by being a part of my journey. I am so grateful for these experiences that have helped me grow both personally and professionally. I have a friend Tom, who those that know both of us joke that Tom is the male version of me. Tom and I met by chance at a conference where our respective employers at the time were exhibiting next to each other. And so it began from there.

Tom is an OD (Organizational Development) guy that went back to his alma mater, Bowling Green State University (BGSU). Tom landed in the perfect role seemingly created for only him! Tom got his ideal role promoting the very program that helped evolve him into an Organizational Development leader. Tom, like me, is a connector. If you have ever read Malcom Gladwell's "The Tipping Point", you will see a picture of Tom and I with crowns. We are the King and Queen of connections and the best collaborators.

I was working on a presentation about five generations working in a multi-generational workplace and how organizations can enhance their total rewards programs to adapt. Tom and I always bounce ideas off each other and after he saw me present it at a conference suggested I read a book by a clinical researcher named Brene' Brown. Brene' has done extensive research on shame and vulnerability and tied it back to employee engagement. Tom shared that someone gave him a copy of one of her books, "The Gifts of Imperfection" and that I needed to read it as research for my presentation. I took Tom's advice, ordered it digitally via Kindle and spent the next 3 hours going to places that scared me. Shame and vulnerability are both words that bring fear and avoidance to many people. There was one chapter that Tom wanted me to see that was relevant to what I was sharing with organizations regarding her research. Employees will be engaged in the workplace if they have the opportunity to have "meaningful work" and "share their gifts". When that doesn't happen or the opportunities are lost – it creates stress. The moment I finished reading "The Gifts of Imperfection", it changed the way I practiced HR forever.

"The only unique contribution that we will ever make in this world is born of creativity". – Brene' Brown

Now Brene' didn't initially engage in her research thinking it would have a profound impact on leadership, HR or employee engagement. HR was probably the last thing she had on her mind when she was taking us all places that we have suppressed and hid. Her subsequent books "Daring Greatly", "Rising Strong" and "Dare to Lead" went there. During the course of reading "Daring Greatly", I think I crawled under the covers, got into the fetal position and had a good cry several times. Vulnerability is a powerful and SCARY thing. Empathy requires vulnerability, both of which enhance the fuel that collaboration needs to thrive.

Brene's insight on the difference between empathy and sympathy emphasizes why empathy is a critical core competency. In short empathy fuels connection on a personal level which enables collaboration, Sympathy prevents or derails that connection as it drives people away.

If you are **not** empathetic, your opportunities to engage in productive partnerships will be limited. When non-empathetic leaders lead, the land of penguins is likely to evolve as collaboration, ideation will be limited and group think is likely to result. Those who can disrupt the cycle leave, give up and grow silent.

Fear and lack of vulnerability typically breed behaviors which create an environment of information hoarding and anti-collaboration. I have encountered this on many different levels and layers in organizations and some organizational cultures thrive on it.

Culture Misfits

I worked on the Agent/Broker side of the insurance industry for over seven years at three different organizations. Agents work on sales and commissions. The cycle from prospect to client is long and built on developing a pipeline of contacts. These contacts can be in name only, lukewarm or via an established referral. The pipeline is critical and managed in most agencies using a Customer Relationship Management (CRM) system like Salesforce. Producers (agents) are very territorial of their pipeline and there are two types of producers - "Hunters" and "Sharks". Hunters continually seek and establish new relationships, manage them and keep that pipeline growing. Sharks swim around and wait for the hunter to do the work. At the opportunity (or when no one is looking), they dive in and claim it as their own.

Anne is one of the BEST and most genuine connectors I have ever met. Her passion to build trust and genuine relationships was accomplished by her ability to collaborate.

When I first met Anne, she was new to the office and industry. She was a great fit for the role due to her drive (a hunter) and her natural ability to collaborate and build genuine relationships. Anne, a peacock with enormous and beautiful feathers, didn't just enter the land of penguins. She entered an ocean that was mostly compromised of blood thirsty sharks.

Every Monday, the producers met to discuss their pipeline and brag about their successes. A well-known and very territorial producer was sharing details on a meeting that she and her team were in the process of trying to obtain with a prospective client. Anne chimed up that she had a long-time relationship with the decision maker as they served on a non-profit board together and asked if she could help with the meeting/relationship. Rather than collaborate with Anne and enhance the value of the relationship (and likely close the sale), the alpha shark immediately went for the jugular - doing so in front of everyone in attendance. It was a vicious territorial display to show Anne that she had no place there and collaboration was not wanted.

In cultures where vulnerability is shunned, fear, insecurity and feeling threatened by partnering with someone for the greater good results in territorial spats and non-professional behavior. This environment fostered and encouraged a competitive culture of "feast or die". Ironically that producer only hurt themselves because they didn't get the client (and with Anne's help, they likely would have had a better chance in closing that deal.) I immediately became of huge fan of Anne for her tenacity and the way she handled that situation. She didn't let this interaction sway her from finding others internally to collaborate with. She became and continues to be one of the top producers in the region and company by embracing collaboration of one of her critical skills to enhance her client relationships.

Empathy also empowers one to be comfortable asking for and accepting of feedback. Feedback is a critical ingredient in fostering a collaborative culture. Where we struggle, is that we are quick to give feedback but struggle in accepting or processing feedback and alternative points of view.

Collaboration is a two-way dialogue between one or more parties to achieve a goal/solution or mutual success. It is not a one-way dictatorship. I have sat in many a meeting where very passionate individuals have very strong views or opinions on the problem/course of action/direction the organization should take. Passion or the drive to "win" (the argument or ego driven need to be right) becomes the biggest barrier to collaboration as it breaks down the opportunities to enhance relationships (or services) through the feedback process. Those naysayers are the anti-collaborators we find ourselves engaged in battle with to try to be open to alternative options and feedback. They highjack the meetings, punish dissention and stifle collaboration. These individuals (which are a plenty) are also the individuals that will ask you for your feedback and when you give it, take it very personal if you don't tell them what they want to hear. They ask you for feedback because in their perspective that is collaborating – but **collaboration requires acknowledgment and acceptance of others views and perspective**. When you treat these types of conversations where opinions differ like a battle, there are no winners only losers. Lost opportunities to be inclusive, innovate and enhance internal strategic relationships and create HR value.

Have you ever sat in a meeting where someone asks your opinion on something and when you give it you feel the wrath like no other?

I worked for a leader who was notorious for this. No matter how constructive, the format of feedback, I found myself regretting giving it. Instead of being engaged in the dialogue, I found myself shutting down in the meeting because dissenting perspectives were viewed as challenging the status quo. In one situation with this leader, I was in a meeting discussing a very dated attendance policy where unplanned absences were tracked over a 12-month period. My counterpart and I were asked our opinion on the policy and I gave constructive feedback that I felt the policy was not consistently tracked and was counterproductive to our PTO policy because it penalized employees for using it. I was quickly provided a defensive response about leadership's unwillingness to engage in modifying the policy (and ultimately felt like I was being scolded for my alternative perspective.). If the organization is not open and accepting of feedback, nor wanting foster an openness to acknowledge alternative points of views collaboration, it will die on the vine. It isn't just the ability to acknowledge, but the capacity to communicate that feedback is ok even when the direction taken may be different. As an HR peacock, I learned from experiences, such as this one, that penguins fear collaboration. The environment was truly the land of penguins.

STOP COLLABORATE AND LISTEN NOTES

6

THE BEAUTY OF ORGANIC COLLABORATION

Sometimes the best lessons on communication and collaboration are provided in the least expected ways. We learn the foundation of "the how" to collaborate during childhood.

My two boys, Kirk and Brent, participate in a national program called Science Olympiad. The program is designed to inspire 3rd through 12 grade students in STEM related areas of study. Science Olympiad tournaments allow students from elementary, middle and high schools to compete in 16 different parent coached events. In addition to individual events, there is also an overall team competition against other schools. Living in Metro Detroit, we are fortunate to have one of the top organized tournaments in the country, thanks to corporate sponsors like General Motors and Detroit Edison.

As a parent coached event, the time investment involved in preparing and attending these tournaments can be overwhelming. Students will sign up to compete and then when the student and/or parents learn how much time is invested in practices, event workshops and tournaments, the team dwindles. Some schools have so much interest and volunteers they can field a main team and an alternate team. The elementary school that my boys attend(ed) usually ends up with 9 kids due to attrition. Therefore, if they want to be competitive in the team competition, students participate in more than the typical two events.

In my oldest son Kirk's first Science Olympiad season, he participated in an event called Reflection Relay. This event requires a 3-4-person team who compete with mirrors, flashlights and lasers to hit targets using refractive light. Teams are given a limited set of time to prepare and discuss their strategy and then work together to make any adjustments to successfully hit a designated target. Kirk enjoyed the event so the next year his dad offered to coach that event with both son's due to lack of volunteers and after the first parent (and associated child) decided to quit. After several attempts of finding the required "3rd" student needed – we advised the schools head coach that we were unable to do the event.

Any school that fails to compete in any individual event is at a significant disadvantage in the team competition. Teams will send individuals into an event if they lack dedicated individuals as participation will result in team points even if the team finishes last. Because he had prior experience, Kirk volunteered the day of the tournament to attempt the Reflection Relay event with two other 6th grade students to avoid the no point penalty. This is where I witnessed true organic collaboration in its finest form.

Reflection Relay has two parts, an A and a B course. Our main tournament is held at a community college campus and due to the scope of this event is held in one of the buildings where multiple teams can compete simultaneously. Parents/coaches can go into the course areas but cannot communicate with the teams.

When my son and his two fellow teammates (both named Emily) arrived to check into the event, I was waived by the three to come in with them. I asked both Emily's if they wanted any of their family to also be present and they said no (I must admit this exclusive invite brought me a rare cool mom moment). So, off I went as the only adult with a group of independent 6th graders who had nothing to lose. As we were escorted to the first course, they were unusually carefree considering they were competing in an event they didn't practice for when everyone else had been practicing for 5-6 months.

The first course included 4 mirrors on a table, a laser and an obstacle. The goal was to bounce the laser off 4 mirrors, around the obstacle and hit a fixed target. All must be done in a 5-minute planning period using rulers/protractors and strategy. This all takes place in a room with 3-5 other teams each navigating the same challenge at the same time. Success requires planning, precision, trust and the true art of collaboration.

When the five-minute timer started, the three of them started to communicate and organically engage in collaborative discussion. Each trusted and respected the input of the others. They were openly sharing feedback when one felt that the ideas/direction of the other were creating roadblocks, they vocalized and worked through the problem. There was no pre-planned agenda, no posturing for control, no information hoarding or shaming for counter ideas. **It was pure and genuine organic collaboration in its finest form.** In five minutes they worked together to identify the problem, discuss workable solutions and establish a course of action – **TOGETHER**. They accomplished a small feat having never competed before or seen the course parameters. The end result - the laser hit all 4 required mirrors and narrowly missed the target (so narrowly that they needed a second opinion to confirm the miss). That narrow miss of achieving full success was all accomplished in a matter of 300 seconds.

In the second part of the course, teams are alone in a dark room. Each team has 1 minute to establish a strategy using a flashlight and 4 mirrors to reflect the light off the mirrors and hit a designated target. This requires precision and collaborative communication in both set up and staging of the hand-held mirrors. Coming off the success of the first part of the course, they engaged the second challenge in the same manner. The difference was the level of feedback shared by all three members of the team during the set up and adjusting process. The first attempt was accomplished in 52 seconds. The second and harder target was accomplished in 13 seconds. The difference in the second attempt was that they learned from failures in the first attempt and adjusted their approach.

They didn't win, but these three 12-year old's displayed communication leadership traits that most organizations struggle to find or leverage. Collaboration in its purest form is fluid, natural and organic. The team finished 20th out of 43 teams. In fact, the difference in their score to that of teams in the top time was mere seconds. Collaboration is a powerful tool to resolve and achieve success as proven by these amazing students. In organizations we tend to be so focused on our own agenda's, opinions or lack willingness to accept alternative perspectives that we miss genuine opportunities to collaborate. Every interaction is an opportunity to collaborate or build trust to enable future collaborative experiences.

My sons continually amaze and remind me of the impacts that collaboration can have on relationships and life. Both of my sons play baseball. They are not your typical hardcore athletes but play for the love of the game. My youngest has a natural ability but is awkwardly shy. My oldest has that "go get 'em" attitude, but as a bigger kid he is awkwardly clumsy. For both of those reasons, we chose to play baseball in a church league where the focus is on developing skills not a career in the major leagues.

First let me say that this doesn't mean there isn't competition. They learn to win and lose with dignity. Trust me, I have sat through some games that were painful to watch but the boys (and girls) all have fun.

I played softball growing up and was a catcher. I loved catching for the simple fact that you get a view of the game no one else gets to see. My boys have both evolved into catchers. Kirk, because of his size as that was one position that he could maneuver well. Brent, because he loves to hustle and no one else ever wants to play that position because you wear a ton of gear, sweat like crazy and have to squat.

Baseball is a team sport in which players must engage in dialogue and the collaborative dance. The Catcher has a very important job to bring the team together when lack of collaboration breaks down and the dance turns into chaos (and it does – A LOT). Catching is a physically hard position that takes time to grow into, which means **mistakes can and do happen.**

It is for those reasons that I was so excited both of my boys embraced a role most kids do not want to do.

At 9/10 and 11/12 years old, kids are just learning how to be comfortable sharing feedback, support and trusting each other. The catcher becomes that voice of calm, leadership and support to encourage and enhance the collaborative spirit on the field. Brent in his shy reserved nature (and safety behind the gear and mask) has started engaging with his team from behind the plate calling plays and reminding them to communicate (and work together as a team). Kirk has become a team leader and helping other kids on the team be comfortable in trusting their fellow team members and finding their own voices.

There are moments in life as a parent that you choke up and think there is hope left in the world. During Kirk's U-12 season (11-12-year old's) in a developmental church league, he was placed on a team that mimicked the "Bad News Bears". In fact, their team colors were yellow and white and if Chico's Bail Bonds could have sponsored them, they probably would have.

The team was comprised of a great group of boys, some of whom had never played before or had some physical challenges. As the luck of the draw would play out, the other teams were stacked with talent. Kirk's team was consistently losing by mercy (10+ runs) per game, but the boys were having fun and embraced each game with motivation. The boys went 1-11 for the season and when they won their one and only game it was like the Detroit Lion's finally won the Super Bowl. It wasn't the fact they won, it was how they won that we can all learn from.

This was a 5-team league and two of the teams were co-ed. In this specific game, we were playing one of the co-ed teams and Kirk was catching. Kirk was having a really rough day. I equate this to both puberty, his DNA, and the fact it was 95 degrees and muggy.

The boys were playing an amazing game and working together. They were finally listening to each other and working together in the field which had been a challenge all season. Our team was down 8-3 through 3 innings but came back in a rally and were up 9-8. This was the most runs they had scored in a game all season and they had <u>never</u> lead before.

As I was sitting in the stands, I heard Kirk yelling words of encouragement to the players in the field from behind the plate. At one point, he told them they had "nothing to lose and everything to gain". He kept yelling words of encouragement and constructive feedback to the pitcher and his team mates to not give up and work together.

Organic collaboration is learned through these experiences where we are comfortable sharing feedback, ideas and working together in a judgement free environment. When we are open to constructive feedback it helps us grow, not hinders experiences and opportunities. What I have learned through the eyes of a parent is that children must have opportunities to learn and overcome adversity when faced with a difficult challenge. The art of collaboration is a powerful tool that evolves from those experiences such as Kirk experienced with his team that season.

STOP COLLABORATE AND LISTEN NOTES

7

COLLABORATION FOR THE SAKE OF COLLABORATION

I worked for an organization that flaunted "collaboration" as a core value yet struggled with genuine organic collaboration. This organization's ideals centered around collaboration had several faults. In short, to them collaboration meant "management and decision by committee" and "meetings". These interpretations of collaboration translated into the organizations management style and culture.

When I was initially interviewing for this particular role, one of the Vice Presidents I met with asked how I felt about meetings. After I shared my perspective about productive dialogue and collaboration, they laughed and said, "Well, we do have a lot of meetings here." I didn't quite understand why they found my response about productive dialogue funny until after I started.

On most work weeks, there were entire days where my calendar was completely booked solid; not due to PTO or outside commitments – but due to 8-9 hours straight of meetings. I would run from one meeting to another which always resulted in me being late for meetings and the nagging feeling of always running behind. This organization was also notorious for scheduling meetings over lunch and meetings over meetings. Overscheduling occurred even when you or your calendar indicated you were not available. I translate that as "Sorry my need is greater to whatever commitment you agreed to before this."

This meeting creep this was not unique to my schedule – so trying to coordinate time to schedule a legitimate meeting with **anyone** was a nightmare. In fact, this process was downright utterly exhausting. **<u>Meeting, for the sake of meeting is NOT collaboration.</u>** Meeting overload completely stifles the organic flow and energy that collaboration has on innovation and partnerships.

There were two additional flaws in this organization's view of collaboration.

The first was its lack of willingness to embrace diversity and inclusion – literally speaking. This organization struggled to accept and be open to alternative ideas and perspectives. As an organization engrained in legacy and traditions, the peacocks were always invited to the party, but always chased out shortly after for disrupting consensus and trying to influence change.

The second was the culture viewed collaboration as a management or decision by committee. Decisions and changes only could be accomplished through engaging and getting buy in from **all** stakeholders. The aspect of this approach can have positive outcomes, if someone takes ownership to make a decision as consensus in this type of environment is hard to accomplish. The result is decisions, specifically, those resulting in change take too long or never happen.

As a self-proclaimed peacock – my time with this organization was short. I am eternally grateful for that time influenced me to speak out on the fact that lack of diversity and inclusion in any organization, team or relationship repels any opportunity for genuine collaboration.

During an interview with a potential employer, I was asked what I loved to do most as an HR professional. You would think this would be a hard question to answer, as one reflects over their professional career to isolate that down to just one thing. But for me it was simple. There are so many things I derive passion from, but one that I find the greatest passion from is organic collaboration. I enjoy the natural dance of generating ideas and openingly sharing thoughts/alternative perspectives that result in accomplishing a task/resolving a problem or creating solutions.

Lack of structure is like kryptonite to HR, so I want to point out to everyone that this free flow generation of ideas does have structure (such as Mind Mapping or the Delphi Technique). I elaborated that the art of this process is truly what drives and inspires me as an HR strategic partner.

My answer was not what the requestor anticipated and honestly, I think they were confused by it. However, my response was genuine. Organic collaboration to achieve its natural state must have peacocks, penguins, pigeons and even some ostriches engaging in the dialogue. The fear and confusion is that engaging in free flow thought cannot result in consensus or produce results. That perspective is indeed a fixed mindset, and one that can keep an organization from achieving its full potential.

Flashback to the organization I was working for at the time that interview question was posed to me. I was working with one of my leaders, Yvonne on a new department structure due to positive changes going on within the team. Yvonne is a high energy and passionate leader who channels that energy in the creation and execution of ideas and concepts. What I loved about working with Yvonne is her energy and desire to be inclusive. Yvonne is open to feedback and embraces the concept of bringing individuals into the process of ideation. These traits make her an amazing collaborator.

We started with the department vision and began working on updates to the job descriptions; from reviewing the current state to the future state. We openly shared ideas and thoughts which evolved into a great vision of where the department had evolved and a revised structure to reflect those changes - all within an hour. It wasn't the time spent to accomplish that was impressive. It was the natural and open flow of ideas and dialogue that allowed that process to happen.

Three days after that session, I was with Yvonne, and her executive and management business unit peers at an offsite all day strategic planning session. During the session there was an ice breaker exercise that asked everyone to write down on a piece of paper what they loved most about the work they do for the organization. I was sitting next to the executive leader of the business unit (to whom Yvonne reports) and shared the collaboration experience from the week prior. Later I shared that thought directly with Yvonne and shared my appreciation for her openness and natural ability to organically collaborate. She shared she was not surprised that I enjoyed that process and that she was looking forward to implementing the deliverable we created. The next day she sent me an email thanking me again for the work with did together and that she truly enjoyed working with me.

We can all reflect on one meeting/discussion/professional interaction on where organic collaboration resulted in a success. My experience with Yvonne is just one example that supports the fact that collaboration builds strategic partnerships.

STOP COLLABORATE AND LISTEN NOTES

8
—

LET IT GO – COLLABORATION DENIED

Over the first half of this book, I have shared insight into the barriers inhibiting us in our ability to collaborate and the many successes that partnership through collaboration brings. Collaboration is something that occurs when each party in the process is open, willing and trusting of the others to engage in ideation, problem solving and failures. There are times when you will show up to the dance, and you wind up being the only one out on the dancefloor. I equate this process like the early stages of dating in High School. Not everyone knows how to dance or trusts that their partner will not drop them or step on their toes.

Every interaction that takes place in our professional roles can ultimately lead to a current or future opportunity to collaborate. Each interaction (even those simple and brief ones) allow us the ability to build trust and credibility with our internal partners – so when they are ready to dance they know we are willing and able to meet them at the center of the dance floor.

Some internal relationships will never be ready or want to engage with HR in the manner we envision the organization needs. For every successful collaborative partnership established, I have had just as many managers or leaders deny or fail to view me outside of a transactional resource. Understanding the needs of those we serve in the scope of our roles allows us to understand when the best opportunities are to take your HR relationship to the next level.

We can't collaborate with everyone at the same time, our plate and scope of responsibilities in our HR lives make that nearly impossible. Therefore, these smaller interactions allow us to meet the needs of our internal partners at that moment in time. We can seize these little interactions to show we are here and ready to dance should the opportunity and need occur. Building trust and credibility takes time. How we approach those small interactions over time helps evolve those relationships into partnerships.

But what about those that we unintentionally avoid – those we choose not to collaborate with? (Remember "that" and "those" managers?) We all have those relationships in life (or professionally) that when you see them calling you – you cringe. These are the managers that are the first to throw you under the bus, always have a fire for you to put out and never thank you for no matter how hard you work to save their world from destruction. I see these types of individuals as the biggest relationship opportunities. Past practice or our natural response to engage these types of individuals is to avoid or seek ways to enact revenge through organizational karma. In my experiences these types of love/hate relationships and taking that vindictive avoidance mindset has only came back to haunt us. These are the leaders and internal relationships which need us the most. As with the story I shared about Anne, we can either let those individuals define how our story is told (and perceived) in the organization or seek every opportunity through action to write our own. Failure to do so, is how HR became known as the land of judgement.

BE PRESENT AND BE SEEN

If you were to ask internal and external business partners what is their perception of HR (how they view us from their line of sight), the general feedback is that HR is not inclusive, accessible and approachable. What does inclusive, accessible and approachable have to do with our ability to collaborate and validate our partnership as being an advocate for the organization?

Taking the traditional HR obsession with structure, process and task orientation out of the equation, let's dive into one of the root causes for the fact organizations think we don't care or want to be bothered. The problem is simple, the problem is us. We fail to be present when engaging our stakeholders and actually be SEEN as a participant in the process, the discussion and ultimately the solution.

Technology has only contributed to this problem. A tactile focused HR mindset is so obsessed with tasks, advancement of tasks and processes that we find ourselves getting deeper and deeper behind the proverbial technology barrier which limits actual human interactions. It is that warm security blanket for so many, that when a problem, issue or question is posed outside of the norm it results in a fear and lack of response. I can hide behind the email or go to my electronic technology happy place, ignore the issue/problem at hand and appear to be doing something of value.

As a parent, the thing that makes me absolute crazy is when I am having a conversation with one or both of my boys who is physically sitting within 3 feet of me and realize they have not heard ONE word I said. As organizations have made technology at everyone's fingertips, the meeting etiquette challenge has resulted around technology distraction. The first step in HR being a strategic partner is being invited to the meeting (be seen). However, we, and a majority of the world today, suck at being "PRESENT". To be present is where the magic happens.

In my journey in writing this book, so many members of our HR Tribe shared stories about how distracting technology has gotten to engaging in productive meaningful conversations in the workplace. Our obsession with technology, immediate gratification and responsiveness to emails, texting and social media have overflowed into our everyday life. This has become an epidemic and why HR in some organizations has become a laughing stock.

When someone engages us in a meeting, conversation or request for assistance, what they value most is:

- Our attention
- Our acknowledgement (active listening – "I understand and recognize …")
- Empathy (non-bias and non-judgmental)
- Trust (that we will process what is shared in a non-judgmental manner and engage with information shared only with those who need to know and not those who don't.)

I worked in an organization where HR stopped getting invited to meetings because they literally just sat in the room without saying a word, head down on a computer or on their phones. In one meeting with several internal business partners, I glanced over, and a counterpart was scrolling her phone on Instagram. I glanced over after I saw several participants doing the same. Ironically, the HR leader was also in the room but failed to notice as she was part of the problem – she didn't have clue as she was doing the same exact thing. The message that this behavior sends to anyone else in attendance is that your time and message/need is not of value and that you are not listening. Just like my boys when I tell them at least ten times every morning to get up and get ready for school – when we fail to be "present" we have tuned out the world both visibly and mentally.

We may not even realize we are behaving this way – partly because we are so process and task focused. The response (excuse) is often "I needed to get this email out to the CEO", "Bruno Mar's tickets just went on sale at 10:00 am." "Princess Kate is in labor!", "OJ just got paroled." The sad fact is that these are all comments that I experienced during meetings which turned non-productive or disruptive because individuals were pre-occupied and distracted by technology and multi-tasking.

This is one of the primary contributors on why there is a stigma that HR (or any professional who behaves this way) is not accessible, inclusive or approachable. Why? Because we openly shut ourselves out in being part of the collaborative process.

As a strategic partner, we are often asked to attend meetings just in case – either to observe or step in if needed. It is easy to fall prey to the multi-tasking drive in all of us and miss critical moments that can create opportunities to collaborate. We can remain engaged in the conversation through eye contact and body language. Our role is unique in that being "in the moment" can allow us to contribute or bring value in ways we didn't anticipate. On a side note, don't speak just to hear yourself talk but you can acknowledge what others are saying or ask questions when appropriate. Be present is the physical representation of active listening and acknowledgment that you are **open** and **ready** to collaborate.

Our failure to be "present" not only results in lost opportunities but a lack of stakeholder engagement and credibility. There are times when life happens, and you need to step out of a meeting, work on an email or item while in a meeting or on a call. These situations should be the exception and not the norm.

In the role of HR, our organizational focus involves serving the needs of many. How we engage and approach these fires when they happen, defines our credibility. Simple rule of thumb is this - when they do, be transparent. Transparency allows you to acknowledge the needs of your audience as important, and at the same time communicate that your attention may be briefly required on another matter. If that distraction is going to be more than brief, eliminate your lack of engagement from being a distraction and politely excuse yourself as appropriate. In the end, your stakeholders respect you more because they know you not only respect their time, but also have a more focused interaction.

Let me share an experience where I was faced with an "HR life happens" moment during a critical period in building credibility with new stakeholders.

I was attending a regional leadership meeting out of town and a significant HR issue began evolving which required my immediate attention. It was one of those "you can't make this "bleep" up" HR moments. We have all had those moments at one or many points during our HR careers.

I was in a conference room with 18 regional leaders and prior to the start of the meeting communicated that there was an HR related time sensitive issue that just came up which required my immediate attention. I then apologized for my pending distraction from the discussion.

The timing for this issue could not have been worse. I was offsite with a high influence cross functional leadership team which I was meeting and engaging with in person for the first time. I was new to the organization and was trying to build credibility with a group that had been apprehensive to partner with HR outside of transactional needs. This first meeting was a pivotal moment for me to build credibility. I was faced with the dilemma to stay present and earn the respect of the leadership team, yet there was no way to avoid this urgent ten alarm employee issue. Completely stepping out of the meeting would play into some of the past frustrations/ lost opportunities that this leadership was vocal about when engaging my department. Since I could not avoid the issue, I chose the only other viable alternative of being transparent and try to minimize the disruption as much as possible. I asked for professional forgiveness prior to the behavior and when the brief distraction was over, I was back and fully engaged in the conversation. I put my laptop to sleep and physically displayed my present status with eye contact and respect for the individuals speaking and presenting. These actions resulted in behaviors that displayed to those leaders attending that meeting that the issues being discussed which were important to them, were also important to me as well.

The issue with this "excuse me" approach is that if you continually engage in excusing yourself from meetings for this reason or using the "HR'ing" excuse to try to multi-task during meetings all the time, internal stakeholders will see right through you. **Trust is earned through action.** Failure to be present and be seen as an active member of the conversation over time will erode any of the credibility you may have had from the times you were.

Mult-Tasking is NOT in the Collaborative Mindset

As humans, we are NOT wired to multi-task when it comes to collaborative processes or life in general. As impossible this unachievable feat is, multi-tasking has evolved into core skill-based competency in nearly every current day job description. The definition of multi-task is to "deal with more than one task at a time". I acknowledge that juggling multiple responsibilities and tasks simultaneously is a professional necessity in every organization. But the million-dollar question is this – <u>Can one effectively collaborate and multi-task at the same time</u>? We brag about our ability to multi-task whenever the opportunity presents itself and we shame those who struggle with it. One of the most overused shaming phrases about the ability to juggle multiple tasks was "You can't walk, talk and chew gum at the same time?" To be honest, I can't and most of the world can't either.

Those guilty of technology distractions, hide behind the excuse of multi-tasking. **Multi-tasking is kryptonite to collaborative discussions.** It prevents active listening (which is pivotal to collaborative dialogue). I used to be a self-proclaimed "multi-tasking master" myself. I thought I could do three things at once. For example, have you ever tried to participate on a conference call on mute, have a conversation with someone in your office and draft an email - all at the same time? I have, and I would hang up the phone and the person would walk out of my office and I would honestly not remember what we talked about because I focused most of my attention drafting that email. We have ALL been there, done that, witnessed that.

Why is it we feel that we can participate and remember everything that is said, or actions taken during a meeting when we focused on other things at the same time? When we do, we are missing all the opportunities for observed stimuli cues (sight/sound) because our focus in a collaborative discussion (or meeting) requires active listening to be able to process the stimuli. When someone attempts to multi-task their focus shifts 1000% to the one or two items they are attempting to do simultaneously and active listening shuts down. When active listening ceases – the siloed focus vacuum consumes your attention and at that point one is simply just "taking up space". We appear non-engaged, non-collaborative and arrogant. Whatever we are working on at the time, which is taking our attention away from the meeting (or conversation at hand) is perceived as more important than the audience to which we are just there "taking up space".

Organizations will only tolerate that behavior for so long before smart leaders will share feedback directly about feeling slighted or simply just "move on".

My husband, Kirk, is a finance guy. When they say opposites attract, they truly meant it, because an analytical financial savvy strategic budget guy married a high flying empathetic passionate people focused HR Master Jedi.

Kirk is the typical audience HR engages at the Executive level C-suite, so I often use his insight as a temperature gauge. I knew I had stumbled onto something worth diving deeper into when we started having a conversation about meetings one summer evening while taking our dog, Tessa, for a walk.

Kirk expressed his observations that organizations are falling into the black hole of non-productive meetings. It isn't often that I can have a work-related conversation with my husband because HR issues are sensitive and financial budgetary processes are not an exciting romantic dinner topic.

I asked Kirk to share with me the rationale behind that comment. He said organizations spend more time having meetings to recap meetings because people are distracted. We may be present in the meeting or logged into the call, but the distractions of multi-tasking (e.g. phones, computers or dual monitors to work on multiple items at once) result in people missing details or the entire concept of any topics discussed or shared. In some cases, rather than have conversations about what transpired in a meeting, we rely on the summary of observations from someone else (e.g. the meeting notes).

Kirk feels that this is resulting into a sense of complacency in organizations and that these behaviors result in lost opportunities for diversity of thought and solutions. If we rely on someone else's perception verses our own, we fail to identify or contribute ideas, thoughts or insight that could have had a direct impact on the organization. Opportunities that are all missed due to multi-tasking and not being "present" in the conversation.

Kirk has identified, from a unique perspective, the determent that failure to be present and seen in meetings has on the organization. It isn't just an HR problem, but it impacts us harder because even though this is an 'organizational' problem. It feeds into the fact that HR doesn't understand or care about the business side of the organization. We need to set the example and the best way to disrupt and be a champion for change is to start one meeting at a time. Opportunities to change perceptions and collaborate will naturally occur because you are creating the right environment for them to happen. Once you have success in one meeting, the next meeting will allow you to build on that momentum and continue to feed new opportunities.

It is amazing how limiting multi-tasking in meetings will lead to higher productivity and less meetings. I used to work with a group of HR colleagues who held the most non-productive meetings on the planet. They were the type of group that would start meetings late and be so easily distracted (e.g. OJ got paroled so let's deflect from the topic to talk about that for 20 minutes). On this team, something that could typically be accomplished in 30 minutes would take three meetings. This team were some of the worst offenders of the glued to the phone, on Instagram or face in laptop experiences I have shared in this chapter. You can likely name at least 5 people right now that all fall into that category. Guessing you may have likely played a round or two of meeting BINGO as a result. Let's all try to be less like them and more in the present!

We have a mission, as HR and organizational leaders to leverage collaboration as one of the important tools in our strategic partnership arsenal.

Don't let fear of the unknown keep you from stepping out from behind your comfort zone. Sometimes the best moments are those you never expected or envisioned.

This is where you begin – and where the magic of collaborative partnerships happens. **STOP COLLABORATE AND LISTEN**

STOP COLLABORATE AND LISTEN NOTES

TINA MARIE'S KEYS TO STRATEGIC PARTNERSHIPS THROUGH COLLABORATION

Embrace EMPATHY

LISTEN First

ASK for and be ACCEPTING of feedback

SPEAK the language of business

Be OPEN minded

AVOID Judgement

Be a "SOLUTIONS provider" not the barrier

Be INCLUSIVE and Be PRESENT

Be ACCESSIBLE

RESPECT and CREATE boundaries

Earn TRUST through ACTION

9

EMPATHY, LISTEN FIRST AND FEEDBACK – THE FIRST THREE KEYS TO COLLABORATIVE PARTNERSHIPS

Embrace EMPATHY

As an advocate of the concept of *Servant Leadership* in human resources and organizations, the concept of putting the needs of others first requires one to embrace empathy.

The ability to acknowledge, understand and share the feelings of those to which we serve allows us to put ourselves in the other person's shoes and position. We do not have to agree with their position, but empathy enables us to avoid judgement and recognize and identify ways to partner to achieve a collaborative solution. It takes the "US vs THEM" approach out of the equation and puts the "Human" aspect back into it.

If we begin to embrace empathy, communicating difficult messages becomes easier. When we do have to communicate a message, which may not be the desired outcome, acknowledging their perspective will result in a respectful dialogue and future collaborative opportunities.

In the movie "Road House", Patrick Swayze's character Dalton held a college degree in philosophy which he incorporated into his role as a head bouncer (security) at various dive bars and drinking establishments.

One of my favorite movie quotes of all time comes from his character and in my professional career (and life) I have made this my mantra.

"I want you to BE NICE – Until It's Time <u>NOT</u> to Be Nice"

Empathy isn't just about "being nice" but approaching those to which we partner with in organizations with empathy allows us to approach dialogue, problems and issues in a manner that results in less hurt feelings and adversary engagement. It encourages us to be nicer no matter how big of an ass the person is on the other end. If you embrace empathy, there are less instances where you must not be nice because you are finding collaborative ways to engage in solutions and not taking sides and passing judgement.

We have all had those moments. You are sitting at your desk trying to work on something when someone keeps calling your extension, then your cell phone and then they email you or just show up knocking at your door. You're annoyed because their call or need is distracting you from doing whatever thing you need to be doing at that very moment.

What you don't know is *why* that person is calling. Maybe they are sitting in the emergency room scared, maybe their plate is full, or they feel defeated after a conversation with an employee or colleague went sideways. It could also be there is an HR related emergency that requires your expertise, knowledge or solution and these calls are a desperate cry for help. You don't know; you're just sitting there annoyed, passing judgement because how dare someone call you when the state auditors have shown up and your team wants to leave to go to lunch.

Empathy starts with leaving judgement at the door. The person calling you or coming to your office has a need – often time just acknowledging that need will allow others to see things from your point of view as well.

Instead of ignoring that person, acknowledge. Often, that one simple step is the solution rather than creation of the problem. Acknowledge that you recognize that their need is important but communicate how and when you will respond. "Hi John, I got your voicemail, I am working on a time sensitive project today, can I reach out to you tomorrow?" or "I understand that this need is urgent – I am in a meeting and can call you in 10 minutes?"

After a presentation on this topic at an HR Conference, I was approached by someone who had attended my session who shared with me her story. Gehan (aka G) shared a brief story on an employee interaction that happened right after my session and how attending it have changed the way she will approach HR going forward. I was very humbled, so I asked her to elaborate why?

Gehan explained that during the session someone was "blowing up her phone". Her normal response would be not to acknowledge or respond until the next day assuming the person would have heard or seen her *out-of-office* message. She decided at the break after my session to listen to the voicemail. The voicemail was from an employee who was just rushed to the emergency room with a health-related issue and was scared and concerned about the sudden need to be absent, benefit coverage and leave of absence coverage.

She called the employee back to provide initial answers and let them know she would follow up with them once she was back in the office tomorrow. The employee was beyond grateful and appreciative. She said if it had not been for my session, she would not have called them back or even responded until the next day at the earliest because there was an assumption that someone else in the department would have handled it.

Empathy creates positive partnerships and a safe environment for diversity of thought and inclusion even during constructive conflict and difficult circumstances.

Every time I sit down with a leader, business partner, employee, I embrace empathy to ensure that I am not forcing my perspectives upon them, that I recognize their points of view, respect their ideas and perspective. Doing so allows us to see things not from 3 feet away but 100 feet out in all directions.

Embrace Empathy – because it is not just about being nice and caring – it is integral for diversity of thought, ideas and trust which frame collaborative partnerships. In today's organization, Empathy is a core competency of any HR or organizational leader.

LISTEN First

Collaborative and strategic partnerships require the ability to control one's natural urge to talk or control a conversation. Have you been in a meeting with a person that talks or says something just to say something (or to make themselves feel smarter?) On the flip side of that, have you sat in a meeting with a person that can't hold back and continually jumps in and interrupts you mid-sentence? Those urges are not necessarily driven by arrogance or control – in most cases it is driven by our excitement and passion for the topic or issue at hand.

When we were in school, "**Listen First**" was driven by classroom etiquette. We were trained from Kindergarten on to raise our hand to speak and to speak only when called upon. In adulthood – and in organizations, it is *"they who speaketh first"* that is often given the floor. We need to get back to a happy medium between Kindergarten and the Boardroom.

Earlier I shared insight on the challenges of being present. If one is "presently" engaged in the conversation, "Listen First" is in full effect. Listening allows us to apply empathy and satisfy our human need to gather data and insight from all possible sources/observations going on around us before we speak. Listening FIRST allows us to be "present" and recognize the needs of our internal customers and bring viable realistic and sustainable ideas and solutions. THIS is what strategic collaboration and partnerships is ALL ABOUT.

Before we are quick to say NO, assume or jump to a conclusion, let's seize the opportunity to allow one of our greatest intellectual senses do its job. Engaging in active listening allows HR to truly gauge what is going on within the internal and external environment to which we do business. It allows us to leverage our expertise in the true manner for which it is intended – proactive support to enhance the organization's strategic vision.

Listening first does not mean you do not engage in the conversation – It creates an environment to showcase your strategic and business inquisitiveness (curiosity) outside of your functional area of focus. Showing interest in the operational areas you support opens so many additional opportunities to partner and enhance your engagement with the organization. Listening even when the conversation isn't strictly about HR initiatives provides us the capability to help organizations eliminate the functional silos which tend to limit perspectives. This makes HR the best *Designated Hitter* in the strategic operational playbook.

Here are several quick steps to active listening to enhance collaborative partnerships.

Be Present

Being present allows acuity of all senses to process and collect data through visual/auditory and other sources that may be missed if other distractions are in play. Multi-tasking just doesn't work.

Think Before Speak

When jumping into the conversation think before you dive in - head first. Contribute to the conversation to provide value not to speak for the sake of speaking. Ask questions in a manner that shows interest but not to distract from the dialogue because you were not present/listening or didn't do your meeting pre-work.

Listen for the sake of LEARNING

Gaining organizational acumen, knowledge and strategic mindset will allow you to better partner with the business to be a proactive and trusted resource.

ASK for and be ACCEPTING of Feedback

We continually coach and encourage leaders that they need to ask for and seek feedback from those they lead on how they can better support the organization and their employees. The irony in that statement is that in many cases we do not practice that same mantra. HR or those within our profession may not appear to be open and receptive to feedback especially when it comes to how we can better service the organization. We can't assume that no news means we are doing great! Some may not be comfortable sharing feedback out of fear (because HR are the judgement wielding – Dept of NO). It is also perceived that if we wanted to know we would ask and since we haven't, we are not open to hearing it. We need to take the advice we provide others on how to engage and ask for feedback. Because regardless how great we think we are - there is always the opportunity to learn and grow.

One SIMPLE Question

Greg Modd, is one of the most dynamic HR Executives I have had the pleasure of engaging and one of the most innovative strategic collaborators that I know. I love my conversations with Greg because he is not only an action-oriented leader – he believes in simplicity when it comes to metrics. During an insightful conversation around engagement, Greg shared a very simple way we can start to ask for feedback and gauge if HR is doing its job. Ask employees one simple question: **Is HR giving you the support and services you need?**

I start by sharing Greg's simple question because asking for feedback is a simple act that we tend to 'over-process' as a process. Let's keep this simple.

If your comfortable asking for feedback – how you accept and acknowledge it will define how genuine and honest the feedback you will receive will be. If you are going to ask for it, you need to be prepared to receive what you may hear. That means avoiding judgement and be sure you are not just asking those who will tell you what you want to hear.

Remember as Brene' Brown reminds us, feedback is only meaningful if the person sharing it is credible and, in the arena, getting their ass kicked with you. There needs to be a filter from true honest and actionable feedback and petty deflections and false expectations. We can do that by asking the right questions to the appropriate audiences.

First, we need to look at our internal customer base as two camps - employee advocate and management advocate. We are not afraid to ask our employees how we are doing. This is a great metric tool which is usually done through a survey mechanism. But what about our internal business partners? Don't assume by asking them from an employee perspective that covers it all because how we service their employee needs is different from a supportive aspect in their managerial roles. Having a real conversation with someone as a follow up to that survey can yield insight and dialogue that the electronic survey may not show.

There are two schools of practicing HR professionals in organizations – tactical and consultative HR. Think of HR as a pendulum – that pendulum is swinging from tactical to consultative through collaborative consulting partnerships. We can help shift that pendulum at the right times by asking our internal business partners how we can better support their business initiatives and adapt our approaches and styles based on their business needs. Our profession needs to find a way to keep the pendulum balanced in the center except for those times that require a temporary shift to one side or the other.

There is not a one size fits all approach to HR. Some leaders may wish to heavily leverage HR as a resource and others just want us there when they need us. We can't take it personally when they only call us when there is a problem. How we approach each interaction or problem is how they will base the next once. Each interaction we have with those we engage in the organization provide the best opportunities to ask for feedback to allow us to make those calls for assistance proactive rather than reactive.

STOP COLLABORATE AND LISTEN NOTES

10

SPEAK THE LANGUAGE, BE OPEN MINDED, AVOID JUDGEMENT

SPEAK the Language of Business

The HR professional language is filled with acronyms, terms and lingo that even those of us who practice it can't remember half of what they all mean. Between laws, metrics, buzz words and the reclusive Narwhal (that is a real thing you know), it is not a shocker that when we start speaking everyone not in HR tune's out. We need to stop assuming the business knows how to speak our language. Rather, let's better understand their language so we can find the right opportunities to integrate our world into theirs.

As a general observation, we absolutely suck at translating what we mean into the general terms that relate to the business for two main reasons –

1. We use command of the HR language as a weapon of organizational power and destruction. (See Judgement Section)
2. We are not able to speak the universal business language of the organization. (See Be Present and Listen First Sections)

As a College Professor, I often struggled with trying to convey the importance of being able to speak in terms that the business can relate to or understand. A traditional student mindset is to quote text –excerpts from a large textbook of many words that they may or may not have read or understand how those "theories" may apply to an organization. They also may not completely understand that the application of said theories will vary based on each unique organizational environment to which HR lives. Part of our professional problem was created during the academic journey many of us took to get here. I personally threw all that out the window for any students that sat through my MBA classes. Before you pass judgement on me, let me share why.

If you walked into a CEO's office and started quoting a text book, theories and or a complete verse from the HR Playbook they would throw you out in two seconds flat. We cannot be so arrogant to believe that organizations hired us to quote and replicate *the way it's always been done*. They hired us to adapt and apply those theories and lessons learned as it relates to the organization at hand. The more we understand the business, the more we can speak and enhance the human capital equation and collaborate on strategy, issues, innovative growth from the HR perspective. We have tried and failed miserably to force managers to speak our language. Let's translate our language and immerse it into the universal language of the organization so it is understood, leveraged and appreciated.

Learn to Speak to a NON-HR Audience

This is a large part of where HR gets a bad reputation. People think we are arrogant and disconnected from the business because we can't speak in general terms. Having the ability to engage in dialogue with any audience at any level builds credibility as an HR partner. The more you can speak in terms a Non-HR person would understand, the more they will seek you out to help because they understand HOW and WHY you can help them!! Big words are scary and can make us look intellectually arrogant, and unapproachable, which is far from our intention. Sometimes we need to use those big words because of risk mitigation but putting the concept into a perspective that makes sense to the audience reflects your ability to connect, build trust and respect with your audience as a true partner and advocate.

Avoid HR Jargon, Lingo and Buzz Words

When engaging your business use common language or terms that will allow the non-HR audience to connect HR concepts and visualize how it impacts or applies to their world as they see it. This does not mean assume that your audience knows nothing (it is possible they don't). By speaking in terms they understand, you not only ensure the audience gets it, but it results in your building trust and credibility as an advocate and partner. Not as the "Entity known as HR".

There are times when it is appropriate and necessary to speak in HR related terms and leveraging the power of your HR voice for the greater good. We need to be mindful to avoid making every engagement with our internal partners about us and trying to educate them to become bilingual and speak the "Language of HR". Rephrasing the language and way we engage, shifts the conversation focus on the organization instead of a struggle to convert every manager into an HR professional.

Seek Opportunities to Learn!

Immerse yourself in the business, industry trends and learn key performance indicators/metrics. Embrace curiosity! Ask questions, make friends with Finance, read the annual report (if you work in an organization that has them), stay aware of external industry emerging trends that may impact not just HR but the organization as whole.

Be OPEN Minded

AVOID Judgement

These are two critical areas which are a work in progress for all of us. If you have read any of Brene' Brown's books you completely understand why. **We. Are. Human.** Humans have emotions, feelings and passion which can enhance or be a barrier to professional interactions.

Where do we start in recognizing the need to act on these two integral aspects of collaborative HR?

EMBRACE DIVERSITY

Diversity is not just about a checkbox for hiring based on outward appearance; it is more about diversity of ideas, thoughts, perspectives and different points of view. For collaboration and strategic partnerships to flourish, approaching issues and ideas without bias (and judgement) is integral for us to gaining credibility as an advocate and partner.

Approaching our role with an open mind requires us to embrace the "OD" (Organizational Development) in all of us and pull off the greatest disruptive intervention of all time. We need to stop hiding behind the "precipitative" and "transactional" way we have practiced HR to begin to swing the pendulum back to the middle and more centered near the "Consultative" and "Collaborative" approach.

LET IT GO

Strategic partnerships and collaboration require the ability to approach situations without judgement. In HR, at the end of the day, it doesn't matter whose fault it is. We must find ways to engage and present solutions. Failure to do so will make that problem evolve into something more heinous over time or become yet a "missed" opportunity for HR to do that "collaborative thing" we have spent an entire book talking about.

Judgement fractures any opportunity to build credible relationships because we just seem to not be able to "let it go". The human side of us often takes things VERY personally. We are strategic advisors, we can recommend and advise but more often than not, a manager or employee turns around and does what they want to anyway. It is not a personal attack on you – it's the fact they are human and made a conscious decision (or deduction) to go in another direction other than the one you suggested. Failure (as epic as sometimes those failures are) are the perfect teachable moments. When we rub salt in the wound and hold grudges then we lose that teachable moment. Remember as a wise one once said …

"FAILURE THE GREATEST TEACHER IS"

Channel passion for a position into opportunities to hear other perspectives, points of view. **It's not about winning**, it's about seeking solutions. If we hold grudges and don't let it go, we will appear unapproachable and that further fuels the Department of No perception.

STOP COLLABORATE AND LISTEN NOTES

11

THE FINAL FIVE

Be a "SOLUTIONS Provider" not the Barrier

Precipitative – Department of No – Policy Yielding Human Resources ... is the HR Department of yesterday. The HR Department of today focuses on collaborative partnerships to enhance strategy. This is accomplished not by disregarding policies but ensuring the policies support the structure and focus the organization needs to grow and operate.

Earlier in the book, I provided several examples of when HR was a barrier, sometimes when we were the ones asking for help or a solution. Becoming a solutions resource takes time. We need to leverage relationships and setbacks to progress. Understanding that there are times when we must say NO, it's the way we communicate that NO that will define if the business is ready and willing to view us differently.

WE WILL WORK THROUGH IT

Solutions require an adequate understanding of the problem at hand, without judgement and an open mind to alternative solutions. My favorite phrase when faced with a Five Alarm HR fire is that "*We will work through it*". Why is this my favorite phrase?

Unfortunately, in most cases we have NO option not to find a way to do so. Regardless of the approach the organization, business, manager took, we may not have agreed or suggested the approach, but we need to do whatever HR needs to do as a result after that decision becomes reality. It's the nature of our role and in some organizations, we spend all day fighting fires (which is absolutely EXHAUSTING!). In those situations, resetting the perception is critical to your HR stamina and existence.

"We will work through it" doesn't mean that we embody the role of "cleaner". If this is the HR life you lead, there are ways you can start helping organizations invite you to the conversation before the decision is made. When we are viewed as a "barrier" to anything and everything – your leaders will not invite you to the party. They will only call you as the option of last resort. This is the reason why the role of "cleaner" occurs.

"*We will work through it*" means that when they do come to you reactively, that we approach that encounter as an opportunity to showcase how we can be a proactive resource.

- Acknowledge the problem and response without judgement.
- Engage as a resource to the resolution.
- Offer alternative solutions (many times the ones we suggested or would have suggested should they have called 1-800-HR first.)
- Use the opportunity to ask if there are any other similar type issues or challenges that you can assist them with (e.g. train them to be proactive and remind the organization you are here when they need you and not just for problems.)

Be INCLUSIVE and Be PRESENT

Inclusion is a critical foundation for collaborative partnerships to thrive. Inclusion places value in the diversity of thought, ideas, perspectives and the points of view of others. When HR is inclusive, it focuses on partnership and a "pull" model of service delivery where our internal business partners (and customers) are engaged in the conversation and feel their needs and perspectives are heard – not judged. Inclusion embodies the ideation process – which showcases HR at its best – being a solutions provider.

We can apply the concept of inclusion and presence in every conversation, meeting, and interaction in the organization. When we are actively engaged in the conversation – providing the individual(s) our full attention, we are mentally and physically present in that moment. Actively listening and focused on the person speaking outwardly portrays that you place value on their perspectives by giving them your full attention and respect.

Technology can be a barrier and distraction to being inclusive and present. The last several keys to strategic partnerships allow you to manage those distractions to enhance the collaborative partnerships based on the dynamics each relationship has with HR.

Be ACCESSIBLE

Being accessible is very personal to me in the delivery of strategic HR. If we, as a profession/entity want to effectively support the organization, HR needs be an accessible resource to both areas of internal customers (Leaders and employees). The centralized HR model as a push service DOES NOT WORK. It may have in the dark ages where we were also called "personnel" but in today's organization it doesn't fit.

The push and pull models are general business models referring to delivery of services. From an HR application of these models, the push is task focused and transactional HR. The pull service model is customizing the core product or service based on customer needs. The pull service model in HR is the collaborative, consultative approach to delivery of HR services. The business units leverage customized HR strategic support in addition to the core services to internal customers.

HR as a pull service model can be centralized as long as it has a footprint in the organization and is visible (and accessible) to employees. Transactional focused interactions contribute to all of the challenges I have described – and make HR less effective as a collaborative strategic partner.

This is about customer service! Every time we go to the grocery store, fly on Delta Airlines, go to a restaurant, take a class/conference seminar or visit a physician – someone is asking us how our experience was and advising us of all the other things they have available if we need it. Maybe HR needs to do that.

In my professional journey I get to meet some amazing champions for our profession. Janelle is a great example on how accessibility allowed her to build credibility and respect with her employees in the field. Janelle in her role as a Regional HR Manager, follows the belief that many of us in the profession portray. The first time someone meets or sees an HR professional should not be the day in which a negative transaction in the employee life cycle is taking place (e.g. performance management, investigation or termination.) Janelle showcases that practice by going out in the field and being visible so when she does need to engage in critical and necessary conversations she is respected and not feared. Janelle believes that HR is "personal" and that we need to not forget that in our service delivery. She signs all employee milestone anniversary certificates and cards within her region because she wants to display the fact that HR is indeed "personal".

In the end, if we are not accessible or hide behind our transactional opportunities to be, how can we impact the experiences within the organization? We can't and we won't. This is our call to action! We need to look outside our four walls, policies and specific areas of focus to see how and where we can be accessible to shine the spotlight that HR is here to partner with you when you need us (and even when you don't!) We need to be visible to our customers to highlight our value and desire to partner.

This is why next aspect of this process is so critical.

RESPECT and CREATE Boundaries

Being accessible will require you to respect the concept of boundaries with those to which you interact. Understanding the demands and needs of your internal partners will allow you the ability to set the "rules of engagement". Once the organization sees the power that collaborative HR has on strategic results, they will all want a piece of the action. For us to be a viable resource for all, we must ensure that we establish a framework that allows us not to be overly consumed to the point of exhaustion – but respected and appreciated. I spoke earlier in the book about trust boundaries. For the sake of this summary, let's put it into the professional expectations to enhance collaborative partnerships.

Setting boundaries starts with acknowledgement of the need/request from the individuals we partner and then prioritizing a response.

I have worked in many organizations where leaders were notorious to email late at night and on weekends. It's 10:30 pm on a Tuesday evening and you are just crawling into bed when you hear that cringing "ding" on your phone that a new email or text has come up. As an on-demand tech obsessed society, we have become hard-wired to respond. Your responding to the email is then interpreted by the sender as "It's ok to send Joe an email anytime because he is up and will respond. Joe needs to now respond to every email I send regardless of the time and his status (e.g. PTO/Sick/ other meetings etc.) because he set the expectation he will respond at any time (day or night)."

JUST SAY NO!

Setting boundaries means you respect the needs of your audience as well as your own needs. Define when you are accessible and kindly remind individuals when you are not. If you are not available, designate someone who can assist in your absence. That means if you are off on vacation – be on vacation. If you tell them you are available if they need – they will need you and not respect your time off because you opened that door. The same goes in consideration for your internal business partners. Respect their time as much as you would like them to respect yours.

Technology

We are addicted to immediate gratification through technology. This addiction causes those traditional professional boundaries to get blurred. Establish the rules of engagement with cell phone access and leveraging your out-of-office protocols in the event you are in longer meetings and not immediately accessible helps. Technology is a big contributor to our distractions yet our biggest opportunity to engage in more effective partnerships by setting those boundaries early.

Technology can also be a barrier or a tool in allowing you to set boundaries. If you are in a meeting and get a message or see an email come in that is urgent, send a quick response back acknowledging their call/email and let them know a timeframe for when they can expect a response. If we don't set those boundaries, the need to satisfy immediate gratification (help me right now) will erode other relationships and your engagements become transactional in nature. Plus, if we keep running from fire to fire, we are unable to provide any true level of partnership. Setting expectations and boundaries allows you to be present for the person you are with yet acknowledge someone else is in need and prioritize the needs appropriately.

Earn TRUST through ACTION

In the last organization I worked prior to taking my passion for Collaborative HR to the next level (and starting my own company), I had the pleasure of supporting the CFO Matt and his associated departments in Finance and Accounting. After I announced my decision to leave (to choose my own adventure), Matt and I were having a conversation about several initiatives we had been working on together to ensure a smooth transition. I thanked Matt for the opportunity to support his leadership and strategic initiatives and for his inclusion as a member of the departmental leadership team. Matt's response summarizes the need for us to approach HR partnerships differently. In short, he said that my interactions and approach not just with him but his entire team resulted in the trust and appreciation as a valued strategic partner.

We can only begin to build strategic and collaborative partnerships by earning the trust of our internal business partners. Trust is earned through action. <u>Each and every interaction is an opportunity to build it no matter how insignificant that interaction may seem.</u>

Leaders need to feel that HR is a safe place to share ideas, issues and seek our guidance. As with setting boundaries, I always treat every conversation in any leadership meeting with the utmost respect. If they share something in confidence, or needed action taken – our approach and response to those actions are what result in <u>trust earned</u>. Trust allows the environment for honest feedback to be accepted, acknowledged and appreciated.

When trust is granted – collaboration thrives. Leaders are more apt to come to you proactively than kicking and screaming later.

Any one of the keys to strategic collaboration shared above can derail the gains in others. But failure to gain trust will be the biggest barrier to any partnership to thrive.

Trust is the biggest tool in your collaborative and strategic HR tool box. The power of trust will allow the value of your partnership to transform as a proactive decision influencer, from being the fixer or denier of progress when things go awry.

STOP COLLABORATE AND LISTEN NOTES

TINA MARIE'S KEYS TO STRATEGIC PARTNERSHIPS THROUGH COLLABORATION

Embrace EMPATHY

LISTEN First

ASK for and be ACCEPTING of feedback

SPEAK the language of business

Be OPEN minded

AVOID Judgement

Be a "SOLUTIONS provider" not the barrier

Be INCLUSIVE and Be PRESENT

Be ACCESSIBLE

RESPECT and CREATE boundaries

Earn TRUST through ACTION

12

MASTERING STRATEGIC HR THROUGH THE POWER OF COLLABORATION

My personal journey in wanting to write this book as a call to action began with a realization that I am not alone. There are many successful champions of HR that have successfully embraced this process. In our world, there are HR Peacocks and organizations who leverage HR as business partnership through collaborative engagement daily with impactful results.

Sometimes it takes a peacock's decision to leave the organization to seek a better flock for an organization to see their value. Some organization's (and traditional HR mindset of precipitative/task focused thought) that are stuck in complacency just never will. We, through our interactions have the ability to control how our story will end. Collaborative HR is merely just the beginning of an evolution that started when someone woke up and said we are more than just administrative doers!

The stories I share in this book are stories not to shame our profession, but to wake us all up from our comfortable complacent policies and silos. Keep in mind that my other claim to fame is my knowledge of compliance. I clarify that as to not have you envisioning my version of HR as a free range parenting free for all in a dystopian society with no rules. There is a magnet on my fridge with a movie quote from the Big Lebowski that reminds all who enter my kitchen of my love for compliance *"Am I the only one around here who gives a shit about the rules?"*

I used to be able to quote sections of regulation at a moment's notice – then I went to HR Therapy and realized that was not necessarily a healthy way to make friends. I just learned to channel the way I share that knowledge differently and when I need to get cozy with my risk management side, I share the "why" a little differently.

HR is not about "Winning the battle or the war on/for/in/at or with Talent" As I embarked on my evolution into collaborative partnerships, I also become more comfortable with embracing who I am professionally and recognizing that as hard as we try, we can't be a disrupter for change alone.

I have spent over twenty-five years in the trenches evolving my craft, learning, trying and failing and doing a LOT of observing. I am far from perfect. Like any human based relationship – the dynamics and the environment which the interactions occur will influence the outcome. Managing it takes patience and effort. Sometimes those reclusive HR behaviors may creep in and try to derail those efforts.

What I have learned when I did have those "fall flat on my face moments" is that it is better to acknowledge failure (and learn from it) then run away and deny it ever happened.

Remember – I mentioned that organizations need a diverse mix of penguins and peacocks to thrive. The traditional HR mindset has primarily been designed and evolved by organizational penguins. We can still embrace our inner peacocks and still embrace, not lose sight of our penguin heritage in the process.

Leadership is not defined strictly by title – but through influence and action. The HR role in every organization should be the outer rim of the wheel, holding and connecting every department and employee asset within the organization together. If we can't learn to approach HR differently and evolve as the dynamics environment of the organizations to which we serve change— those spokes will become siloed, bent and eventually break off.

WE ARE BETTER TOGETHER

We have a mission to start listening to the needs of the business and finding ways to enhance the organization through our power of knowledge, expertise and influential leadership. We see things not just from 10 feet in front of us, but 100 feet out in all directions. We are advocates to all of our internal customers, management and our greatest employee assets. Our organizations need solution providers and strategic innovators. Let's give them what they need!

STOP COLLABORATE AND LISTEN

STOP COLLABORATE AND LISTEN NOTES

BIBLIOGRAPHY

Brown, Brene' (2010), *The Gifts of Imperfection –Let Go of Who You Think You're Supposed to Be and Embrace Who You Are,* Hazelden Publishing

Brown, Brene' (2015) *Daring Greatly: How the Courage to Be Vulnerable Transforms the Way We Live, Love, Parent and Lead,* Avery Publishing Group

Brown, Brene' (2015) Rising Strong: How the Ability to Reset Transforms the Way We Live, Love, Parent and Lead, Spiegel and Grau

Brown, Brene' (2018) *Dare to Lead: Brave Work. Tough Conversations. Whole Hearts.,* Random House Publishing

Gallagher-Hateley, Barbara and Schmidt, Warren H, (2015), *A Peacock in the Land of Penguins: A Fable About Creativity and Courage,* Berrett-Koehler Publishers

Keller, Gary and Papasan, Jay (2013), *The One Thing: The Surprisingly Simple Truth Behind Extraordinary Results,* Texas, Bard Press

ABOUT THE AUTHOR

Tina Marie Wohlfield is the founder and Chief People Strategist at TIMAWO (pronounced Tee-ma-woe). She is a passionate champion of Human Resources, Leadership and Talent Management with over 25+ years' experience in the Human Resources profession.

Tina Marie received her MBA with a concentration in Human Resources Management from Walsh College and holds both the Senior Professional in Human Resources (SPHR) and SHRM Senior Certified Professional (SHRM-SCP) certifications. Tina Marie is an active member of the HR community and dedicated advocate for advancing the HR profession through collaboration, partnerships and mentorship. In 2018, she co-founded HRUnite!, a professional networking and advocacy group to support and advance the HR profession through impactful professional relationships.

Tina Marie is a frequent speaker on HR and leadership topics and an instructor of Human Resources related programs at Walsh College (Troy, MI) since 2008.

Tina Marie currently resides in Fraser, Michigan with her husband Kirk, two boys (Kirk Jr and Brent), two cats (Bailey and Princess) and a rescued Puerto Rican Sato Dog named Tessa.

TIMAWO Company Logo

For additional information on #TEAM TIMAWO, including speaking or organizational engagement opportunities visit:

www.timawo.com
email - info@timawo.com

TESTIMONIALS

I'm reminded of how truly special Tina Marie is every chance I get to work with her. She has a passion for HR and connecting people that I have rarely come across. I've worked with her now for several years and can always count on her to bring that level of passion and energy in everything she does. So happy that her book has become a reality and I can't wait for everyone to read it! – **Paul Sherwood**

As an HR professional, we are often tasked with helping others with overcoming challenges and decisions. The best HR professionals not only do this with those that they support, but all they come in contact with.

Tina Marie is no exception. As an individual, her energy and desire to support and celebrate the strengths of all she comes in contact with are immediately noticed, but her vulnerability to further share her story and path in this book to further advance the profession are greatly appreciated.

During a time of self-reflection and redirection, this book spoke to me personally.

When I first decided that HR was my passion and purpose, I was energized by the idea of working between the business and employees to drive results and engagement. After years of experience, I have found that it is this is imperative to organization success, but difficult to achieve for many reasons. Personality plays a dominant role in our perception of workplace satisfaction and how we are received by others, but Tina Marie validates the importance of staying true to our inner "peacock" and embracing the journey that defines each individual as an HR professional. Tina Marie truly gets it, and I would recommend this book to anyone that is looking to begin a career in HR, to the most seasoned professionals looking for the hope and confidence to make a difference. – **Jennifer Dupont**

Peacocks are colorful. Peacocks stand out. Peacocks make every aspect of life better and more captivating.

Tina Marie is just that. She is a Peacock; that IS her trademark. What I love most is how Tina Marie can lead people and cultivate an incredible following by being real, dynamic, always teaching, connecting and helping. A true Peacock, a true HR Professional with more than something to say. Her stories and the way Tina Marie articulates her message is clear, relevant and always with a flair that proves to assemble a standing room only venue when she speaks at events.

So proud and happy to have built an incredible friendship. This book is only the start. – **Anne Young**

"Tina Marie is a unique HR talent. Always insightful with a strong pro-active approach to her proven methods. Having such a deep think-tank mentality has kept her the most important resource in my HR network" - **John Kontos**